THE BIGGEST BIG HAIR BOOK of METAL TRIVIA

1001 HEAD BANGING QUESTIONS

Ron Higgins
Don Higgins

Small Town Girl Publishing

Library of Congress Control Number: 2022949829
Cover Design by: Purple Penguin Designs

For information please contact:
Small Town Girl Publishing
www.smalltowngirlpublishing.com
ISBN: 979-8-9863305-6-3

We dedicate this book to our parents, Harold and Dolores, and our amazing kids, Carter, Hannah, Rylie, Ethan, Evan, Zane, Chase, Jack and Aiden.

We also dedicate it to all of the "big hair" artists and fans around the world, despite what they may have inadvertently done to the ozone layer.

TABLE OF CONTENTS

PREFACE

You can call it hard rock, heavy metal, hair metal, or glam rock. It doesn't matter what you call it, you know what we're talking about. Screeching vocals, pounding drums, screaming guitars, thumping bass lines. They're all pretty good descriptions with one exception. Big Hair. Somehow, this one seems to be the most popular and has really taken hold for people describing this music. Some people even sink low enough to write books using Big Hair in their title. Shameless. The problem, of course, is that "big hair" has been synonymous with rock and roll for *every* generation, not just the '80s. Even the Beatles were considered to have too much hair when they first became popular. Yes, it's true that lots of '80s artists had big, pretty hair. But many rockers of the time had little to no hair. **Brian Johnson** and **Klaus Meine** didn't have a ton of hair. And **Udo** had almost no hair while **Chris Slade** didn't have *any* hair. Yet all of this music is considered Big Hair. Nevertheless, the term "Big Hair" has come to represent this great music, so let's just go with it. Besides, we're hoping for a nice kickback from Aqua Net. Or Rogain. We don't discriminate.

Although we love all kinds of music, we've always held a special place in our hearts for this bombastic, hard rock music that provided the soundtrack to our younger years. We truly were **Youth Gone Wild.** It started when we bought our first album, **KISS** *Alive II.* Junior High was all about a little band out of Australia known as Air Supply. Would you believe Olivia Newton John? The Wiggles? As you probably guessed it, was **AC/DC.** In 1980, they released their monster album *Back in Black*, featuring former **Geordie** vocalist, **Brian**

Johnson. Once we hit high school, hard rock was really hitting its stride thanks to popular albums by **Van Halen, Quiet Riot, Ratt, Def Leppard, Iron Maiden, Ozzy, Motley Crüe** and the like. And yes, **KISS** was still going strong too, introducing the interesting new gimmick of *not* wearing makeup. During our college years, hard rock was still dominating the airwaves and MTV. It was the days of the "W" bands: **Warrant, Winger, White Lion,** and **Whitesnake.**

Our obsession for rock and roll has seen us invest roughly the GDP of a small nation by forking over countless sums of money for CDs, DVDs, cassettes, and videos. Believe it or not, we even have an 8-track of *Love Gun* by **KISS**. Yes, an 8-track. We've also spent tons of money attending hundreds of concerts. Unfortunately, the days of $12 tickets and $10 T-shirts are long gone. We gave up our concert virginity in 1983 when we saw **AC/DC** in concert on the North American leg of the *Flick of the Switch* tour with **Fastway** opening up. Like the true rock-obsessed music aficionados we are, we have kept all of our ticket stubs. Thrown into this collection is numerous guitar picks, drumsticks, and set lists we've managed to snag while rushing the stage in death-defying maneuvers to obtain a memento before some steroid-induced security guard with too much testosterone starts chalking his knuckles. We've also been fortunate enough to meet quite a few of the artists who make their living at this game, such as the **Scorpions, Dio, Symphony X, Winger, House of Lords, Pretty Boy Floyd, Jackyl,** and others. And then there was the time we met **Quiet Riot.** But more on that story in the pages ahead.

Our music obsession took another leap forward nearly twenty years ago when we started transcribing interviews for the immensely popular **melodicrock.com**. We've also been staff writers for **Hardrock Haven**. We've reviewed many new albums by artists like **Ace Frehley, Krokus, Saxon, Kix, Europe, Rhinobucket, Stratovarius**, and others while writing concert reviews for the likes of **Night Ranger.** We've also conducted interviews with **Bret Michaels**, as well as members of **Tesla, Great White, Dokken, Warrant, Dangerous Toys, Steelheart,** and **Joe Lynn Turner.** Though not metal, we were fortunate enough to interview legendary **YES** front man, **Jon Anderson**.

Due to our **Extreme** love of hard rock, we decided to write this trivia book. We did a lot of research using the internet, but we also referenced many books, magazines, radio interviews, television programs, and anything else we could find related to hard rock and metal. Needless to say, sifting through the mountain of information was no small task as its colossal size was roughly that of **David Lee Roth's** ego. But sift through it we did, and we have come up with 1,001 hard and heavy questions to challenge any resident head-banger. But be warned, we know our stuff. We even "stumped" Eddie Trunk. Twice. So don't feel bad if you don't know all of the answers. We are professionals!

INTRODUCTION

"I Wanna Rock!" "I Love Rock and Roll." "Rock & Roll Ain't Noise Pollution." "Rock You Like a Hurricane", "For Those About to Rock", "Rock 'N' Roll Children". What do these all have in common? Not only do they all have the word "Rock" in them, but they're also great songs by hard rock/heavy metal bands that were hugely successful in the '70s, '80s and '90s. And lucky for us, one of the greatest genres in musical history has also supplied us with some of the most fascinating pieces of trivia this side of **Slash's** top-hat–like, **Slash's** real name. Do you know it? It's very impressive if you do. But if you don't know his rather biblical name, don't fret, most of the questions in this book are multiple choice. Each multiple choice question has four choices, but let's just say one of the answers is pretty obviously incorrect. You shouldn't have any problem figuring out which one it is. For example, *Saving Ryan's Privates* is definitely *not* the answer to one of the questions in the Movies chapter! So basically you've got a one in three chance of choosing the correct answer, which is far better than the odds of **Ace** or **Peter** rejoining **KISS** for the tenth time.

Not every question is multiple choice, however. Several chapters contain matching sections where you match items together, like matching bands to their respective singers or matching the original artists of famous metal cover songs. The matching questions don't have any incorrect answers, but they're a lot of fun because some of the matches are pretty easy and others, well, not so much. If you can match all of the questions correctly, then you're a true metal master, worthy of shooting **Ted Nugent's** crossbow or swinging a **Manowar** broadsword. We're pretty confident you won't be able to though. Some of these questions are expert level, and you basically have to eat, sleep, and drink metal. Or at least be able to bend it with your teeth like **Thor**. So grab your favorite beverage, crank up some ear-splitting rock, and get ready to test your heavy metal aptitude.

It's time to Rock!

CHAPTER 1
BLOW UP YOUR VIDEO

Musically, the Eighties will be forever remembered as the decade that gave us MTV. Although music television shows were around before MTV hit the scene (remember *Don Kirshner's Rock Concert* or *The Midnight Special?*), the new cable channel brought a whole new dimension to music. Having a good song was now only part of the success formula. You also had to have a good video. For some bands, their videos were probably the only reason we've ever heard of them. Videos for hair metal bands were mandatory. How else could young girls see the flowing, golden mane of White Lion's Mike Tramp or know the sexiness that was Lemmy?

1. Which Def Leppard video contained footage of a cartoon which began... "On his quest for the unique woman, Def Leppard chances upon the ominous planet Doom where he spies an unusual procession...?
A. "Armageddon It"
B. "Women"
C. "Animal"
D. "Little Women"

2. Which Van Halen video features David Lee Roth as Napoleon, Michael Anthony as a Samurai warrior, Alex Van Halen as Tarzan and Eddie Van Halen as a cowboy to save an attractive woman from being molested by midgets. No, seriously.
A. "(Oh) Pretty Woman"
B. "Unchained"
C. "Atomic Punk"
D. "Big Bad Bill (is Sweet William Now)"

3. Before she teamed up with Ozzy, Lita Ford had a popular song and video from the early '80s where she changes from an ordinary housewife to a guitar wielding metal woman who beats up a group of burglars. Name the song/video.
A. "Back To The Cave"
B. "Kiss Me Deadly"
C. "Gotta Let Go"
D. "I Wanna Swiffer!"

4. Which Scorpions video features black cats and women with red bars painted across their eyes as the band performs inside a cage with fans rocking it back and forth. No, really... that was the video.
A. "Rock You Like a Hurricane"
B. "Still Loving You"
C. "Big City Nights"
D. "Siegfried & Roy Rocks!"

5. Dokken were fittingly seen riding on a fire engine in the video for which of their songs?
A. "Burning Down the House"
B. "Paris Is Burning"
C. "Burning Like a Flame"
D. "George Burns"

6. What song did Metallica finally decide to make into their much anticipated first video?
A. "One"
B. "Master of Puppets"
C. "Enter Sandman"
D. "Sell Out"

7. The boys from Stryper fly in their own personal black and gold helicopter at the beginning of which video?
A. "Calling On You"
B. "Always There For You"
C. "Free"
D. "Flight of the Bumble Bee"

8. Which Judas Priest video portrayed the band as guitar-wielding bank robbers who successfully break in to retrieve one of their gold records?
A. "Breaking the Law"
B. "Parental Guidance"
C. "Hellion"
D. "Back On The Chain Gang"

9. What popular Van Halen video featured younger versions of the famous band?
A. "Hot for Teacher"
B. "Unchained"
C. "Jump"
D. "Hot for Kreacher"

10. The actor who played Flounder in *Animal House* reprises his role uttering "Oh boy is this great!" while spraying water on his nemesis in which classic metal video?
A. "We're Not Gonna Take It"
B. "We Rock"
C. "I Wanna Rock"
D. "Shout"

11. Name the Dokken video where the band is being chased by an angry mob and they pass a graffiti painted wall with "PMRC" written on it.
A. "Prisoner"
B. "The Hunter"
C. "In My Dreams"
D. "Run Away, Run Away!"

12. Which Ronnie James Dio video has him strutting on rooftops while his band saves a female from her stalker with their loud metal attack?
A. "Rainbow in the Dark"
B. "We Rock"
C. "Mystery"
D. "Ronnie James Dio on a Hot Tin Roof!"

13. Who was the original host of MTV's *Headbangers Ball*?
A. Adam Curry
B. Kevin Seal
C. Riki Rachtman
D. Barbara Walters

14. What Ozzy video featured Frank Zappa's son Dweezil?
A. "Shot in the Dark"
B. "Bark at the Moon"
C. "Rock 'n' Roll Rebel"
D. "Don't Eat the Yellow Snow"

15. Which Motley Crüe video features wrecks of dragsters and speed boats?
A. "Rattlesnake Shake"
B. "Dr. Feelgood"
C. "Kickstart My Heart"
D. "The Malachi Crunch"

16. Y&T helped transform a total nerd into a dashing young man so he could "get the girl" in which of their videos?
A. "Summertime Girls"
B. "Contagious"
C. "Lipstick and Leather"
D. "Groovy Grubworm"

17. Which famous AC/DC video featured a bunch of rockin' Angus clones?
A. "Who Made Who"
B. "Back in Black"
C. "Money Talks"
D. "Angus & Butthead"

18. Which Quiet Riot video starts out in a hospital ER and then shows their famous "mask" singing?
A. "Cum on Feel the Noize"
B. "Slick Black Cadillac"
C. "Mama Weer All Crazee Now"
D. "Marcus Welby, M.D."

19. What did the school kid proclaim that he "wanted to do with his life" in a popular Twisted Sister video by the same name?
A. "Rock & Roll"
B. "I Wanna Rock"
C. "Stay Hungry"
D. "Drink Beer, Drop Out of School & Become a Loser!"

20. What does the woman in the beginning of David Lee Roth's "Yankee Rose" video say when the clerk pops a breath mint and seductively says, "Our lips are so close"?

A. I'm trying to find a laxative!

B. Not if you was the last immigrant grocer on Earth, honey!

C. Not on your life, fool!

D. I wouldn't kiss me because I've got a lip fungus they haven't identified yet.

21. Which Kix video from their 1983 album *Cool Kids* featured the band rocking out while high school girls exercised in their school gym?

A. "Same Jane"

B. "Body Talk"

C. "Sex"

D. "Physical"

22. What was the first video released from David Lee Roth's sophomore solo LP which showed him rock climbing and riding a surf board?.

A. "Just Like Paradise"

B. "Damn Good"

C. "Skyscraper"

D. "Cowabunga, Dude!"

23. Name the KISS song whose video ends with a girl peeking at the band as they get dressed in hopes of seeing them without their makeup, only to discover that they were all dressed in street clothes but still wearing their face paint?

A. "Hard Times"

B. "Dressed to Kill"

C. "Shandi"

D. "Peeping Ace"

24. What Guns N' Roses song won MTV's "Best Heavy Metal Video" award in 1989?
A. "Paradise City"
B. "Welcome to the Jungle"
C. "Sweet Child O' Mine"
D. "Axl's Late, Again"

25. What was the only KISS video to feature the late, great guitarist Mark St. John?
A. "Animalize"
B. "Heaven's On Fire"
C. "Tears are Falling"
D. "Kumbaya"

26. Which Dokken video features the band performing in a graveyard?
A. "Heaven Sent"
B. "In My Dreams"
C. "The Hunter"
D. "Ghost in the Graveyard"

27. Which classic Faith No More video caused a lot of controversy by showing a fish out of water flopping around?
A. "Epic"
B. "Falling to Pieces"
C. "The Real Thing"
D. "The Incredible Mr. Limpet"

28. In the beginning of Poison's video "Nothing But a Good Time", Poison is heard on the radio doing a cover version of what classic rock tune?
A. "Rock and Roll All Night"
B. "Rock & Roll"
C. "Walk This Way"
D. "Delta Dawn"

29. Ted Nugent portrayed a coal miner in the video for what Foreigner sounding '80s song?
A. "Don't You Want My Love"
B. "Blame it on the Night"
C. "Tied Up in Love"
D. "Blame it on the Rain"

30. Which Twisted Sister video featured the band not wearing makeup and a hot girl drag racing and washing a car?
A. "The Price"
B. "Hot Love"
C. "We're Not Gonna Take It"
D. "Car Wash"

31. Which Motley Crüe video begins with a Doberman snatching a kid's homework?
A. "Smokin' in the Boy's Room"
B. "Girls, Girls, Girls"
C. "Wild Side"
D. "Kibbles N' Bits"

32. Which Ratt video ends with a hot woman telling Groucho Marx that men are following her and he replies sarcastically, "'Really? I can't understand why."
A. "Lack of Communication"
B. "Body Talk"
C. "You're in Love"
D. "867-5309"

33. Name the Def Leppard video which was filmed at a traveling circus.
A. "Pour Some Sugar on Me"
B. "Animal"
C. "Hysteria"
D. "Pour Some Elephant Dung on Me"

34. Which Bon Jovi video begins with Sam Kinison soliciting the help of fans to create their own Bon Jovi video?
A. "Bad Medicine"
B. "You Give Love a Bad Name"
C. "Livin' On a Prayer"
D. "Squidward in a Chair"

35. Which Ozzy video features two heavily made up look-alike little girls and a boa constrictor?
A. "Mama, I'm Coming Home"
B. "Mr. Tinkertrain"
C. "Crazy Babies"
D. "Imitating Alice Cooper"

36. Who was the famous comedian that appeared in Twisted Sister's video "Leader of the Pack"?
A. Sam Kinison
B. Bobcat Goldthwait
C. Gilbert Gottfried
D. Marlon Brando

37. Which Whitesnake video ended with a car crashing through a barricade, falling off of a roof and ending in a fiery explosion?
A. "Fool For Your Loving"
B. "Slow and Easy"
C. "Slide it In"
D. "The Middle Pedal's the Brake?"

38. Lita Ford does her take of *Alice in Wonderland* in which video?
A. "Hungry"
B. "Kiss Me Deadly"
C. "Back to the Cave"
D. "Don't Come Around Here No More"

39. Which pre-comeback Aerosmith video from the '80s focused on fans filming bootleg videos of the band in concert?
A. "Sweet Emotion"
B. "Walk This Way"
C. "Let the Music Do the Talking"
D. "Let the Muzak Do the Humming"

40. Which Britny Fox video began as follows: A homeless guy presses a button next to a TV with a sign that says "Press Here" and the band appears and starts singing?
A. "Long Way to Love"
B. "Girlschool"
C. "Dream On"
D. "Let the Sunshine In"

41. What Pretty Boy Floyd video starts with mobsters with Tommy guns shooting 'Rock & Roll' into a wall & then the band appears behind the wall with guitars in place of guns?
A. "48 Hours"
B. "Rock N Roll (Is Gonna Set the Night on Fire)"
C. "I Wanna Be With You"
D. "C is for Cookie"

42. What band's video for "Boyz are Gonna Rock" may possibly be the cheesiest metal video of all time, culminating with the entire band trashing their instruments on stage, the lead singer thrusting his guitar into a large amp and some fool jumping off of one of the amp stacks after he has been set on fire?
A. Vinnie Vincent Invasion
B. Frehley's Comet
C. Aerosmith
D. Deputy Dawg

43. Name the nerdy kid in Van Halen's "Hot for Teacher" video.
A. Waldo
B. Willy
C. Bernard
D. Spaz

44. What heavy metal band won MTV's 1988 Music Video Award for "Best New Artist"?
A. Slaughter
B. White Lion
C. Guns 'N Roses
D. The Crickets

45. Which Judas Priest video features the band, as well as a robot with a skeleton head, riding motorcycles throughout it?
A. "Breakin the Law"
B. "Heading to the Highway"
C. "Turbo Lover"
D. "Hecks Angels"

46. Name Twisted Sister's popular song and video which caused the PMRC to get upset at the image of the teenager "beating up daddy".
A. "The Price"
B. "I Wanna Rock"
C. "We're No Gonna Take It"
D. "Momma Said Knock You Out"

47. Name the legendary comedian who appeared in Ratt's debut video "Round and Round".
A. George Burns
B. Milton Berle
C. Bob Hope
D. Freddy Kreuger

48. In the Judas Priest video for "Locked In", what edible treat does Glenn Tipton use to help rescue Rob Halford from his underground captors?
A. A King Don
B. A Twinkie
C. A Ho-Ho
D. A Brontosaurus Burger

49. What was the name of the model who appeared in Warrant's famous video "Cherry Pie"?
A. Lucy Brown
B. Lacy Brown
C. Bobbie Brown
D. Lucy Van Pelt

50. What was the name of the station wagon in which the girl drove off the cliff in Twisted Sister's "Leader of the Pack" video?
A. Rainy Night
B. Go Slow
C. Caution
D. Thelma & Louise

51. What Motley Crüe video features Latin American gang-bangers buying drugs?
A. "Don't Go Away Mad (Just Go Away)"
B. "Kickstart My Heart"
C. "Dr. Feelgood"
D. "West Side Story"

52. What 1971 movie supplied the basis for Metallica's hit video "One"?
A. *Apocalypse Now*
B. *Johnny Got His Gun*
C. *Hamburger Hill*
D. *Johnny Dangerously*

53. What happens to the man checking noise levels in the Judas Priest video "You've Got Another Thing Coming"?
A. His ears fall off
B. Steam comes out of his ears
C. His head explodes
D. His butt falls off

54. According to the classroom blackboard, what classical musician were the girls prepared to study in the video for Britny Fox's "Girlschool"?
A. Beethoven
B. Mozart
C. J.S. Bach
D. Guinness Stout

55. Name the former secretary who starred in Sam Kinison's "Wild Thing" video.
A. Donna Rice
B. Gennifer Flowers
C. Jessica Hahn
D. Betty Boop

56. The Scorpion's big hit and video "No One Like You" was shot in part at what famous jail?
A. San Quentin
B. Alcatraz
C. Leavenworth
D. San Francisco

57. Who was the most identifiable, tattoo-covered host of MTV's *Headbangers Ball*?
A. Riki Rachtman
B. Alan Hunter
C. Mark Goodman
D. Buck Naked

58. According to the banner she was wearing in the "Hot For Teacher" video, what title did the hot teacher hold?
A. Ms. Hottie
B. Ms. Chemistry
C. Ms. Academic
D. Ms. Sissippi

59. What classic arcade game is playing at the beginning of the Judas Priest video "Freewheel Burning"?
A. Turbo
B. Pole Position
C. Spy Hunter
D. Minecraft

60. In the futuristic video for Queensrÿche's "Queen of the Reich" what are the band members referred to as they battle the evil queen?
A. The Ryche
B. The Five Freedom Fighters
C. Nightriders
D. The Foo Fighters

61. What does the kid say at the end of the video for Motley Crüe's "Smokin' in the Boy's Room"?
A. Rock & Roll baby
B. That's what I'm talking about
C. Now maybe they'll see my side of things
D. Whatchu talkin' 'bout Willis?

62. Who is driving the car at the beginning of Motley Crüe's video for "Kickstart My Heart"?
A. Chevy Chase
B. Tommy Lee
C. Sam Kinison
D. Roscoe P. Coltrane

63. At the end of Poison's "Unskinny Bop" video, what did the sign say that the two female groupies hung on the door as they pulled C.C. back in through the door?
A. Beware of Dog
B. Do Not Disturb
C. Private Session
D. Beware of C. C. Banana

64. What heavy metal video ends with the warning, "Coming Soon to a Beach Near You"?
A. Sammy Hagar's "Mas Tequila"
B. Great White's "Once Bitten, Twice Shy"
C. Shark Island's "Bad For Each Other"
D. Jan & Dean's "Ride The Wild Surf"

65. Which Judas Priest video ended with the disclaimer "Warning: The Surgeon General has determined that Heavy Metal is dangerous to your health"?
A. You've Got Another Thing Coming
B. Freewheel Burnin
C. Spin Out
D. Strip Poker

66. What's the name of Bret Michael's motorcycle as seen in Poison's video for "Fallen Angel"?
A. Hollywood Taxi
B. Bret's Bike
C. Rocket Ride
D. Timmy's Tricycle

67. In the Ratt video for "Wanted Man", which member got shot at the end of the video but caught the bullet in his teeth?
A. Juan Croucier
B. Stephen Pearcy
C. Bobby Blotzer
D. Trigger

68. Who chases Twisted Sister in their video "You Can't Stop Rock and Roll"?
A. The Police
B. The Taste Squad
C. The Army
D. The Mod Squad

69. In David Lee Roth's "Yankee Rose" video, what does the savage (a.k.a. Roth) tell the sales clerk he wants in addition to a "bottle of anything"?
A. A Glazed Donut
B. A Fifth of Whisky
C. Tic-Tacs
D. Feminine Hygiene Products

70. What adult film star appeared in the Helix video for "Gimme Good Lovin'"?
A. Jenna Jamison
B. Ron Jeremy
C. Traci Lords
D. Marge Simpson

71. Although *Headbangers Ball* finally returned to the airwaves in 2003, it didn't reappear on MTV. Which network did it appear on?
A. MTV2
B. VH-1
C. VH-1 Classic
D. Cartoon Network

72. What was the name of the clown in the beginning of Ratt's video for "Lay it Down"?
A. Chucky
B. Chucko
C. Zippy
D. Krusty

73. At the end of Cinderella's video for "Somebody Save Me", two groupies yell, "There they are!" but run right past members of the band to two other rockers. Who were they?
A. Jon Bon Jovi & Richie Sambora
B. Stephen Tyler & Joe Perry
C. Vince Neil & Tommy Lee
D. Lucy & Ethel

74. Whose video "Falling In and Out of Love" features the singer wearing a pair of "Daisy Dukes" and repeatedly spanking her butt in a desperate attempt to look sexy?
A. Femme Fatale
B. Lita Ford
C. Vixen
D. Wilma Flintstone

75. Motorhead's video "Hellraiser" features an epic battle between which foes?
A. Motorhead vs. Pumpkinhead
B. Motorhead vs. Pinhead
C. Motorhead vs. Freddy Krueger
D. Tiffany vs. Debbie Gibson

Hanging with
LA Guns

CALLING POISON CONTROL

Poison is arguably one of the greatest glam metal bands to ever apply makeup, spray on copious amounts of Aqua Net, and strap on guitars. So conducting a phone interview with their singer, Mr. "Rock of Love" himself, Bret Michaels, was both crazy and surreal. As with most things worth pursuing, it took a little luck, some hard work, and a dash of "who you know."

Bret Michaels was in the studio of our local radio station promoting his show in town that night. Not content to just transcribe interviews for our buddy Andrew's website, we decided to interview him ourselves! So we called up the radio station and asked to speak with Mr. Michaels. Simple, right? Wrong! Although he had been in the studio previously, a lot of the interview had been pre-recorded. He and his entourage were long gone. Not willing to throw in the towel quite yet, we explained to the DJ we simply wanted to get in touch with him to do an interview for the website. Much to our surprise he gave us the contact number for Bret's PR firm. And just like that, we had access to the platinum selling artist who gave us such hits as "Nothin' But a Good Time," and "Every Rose Has Its Thorn."

Working with his rep, we set up a phone interview and patiently waited for the day to conduct it. Not wanting to give out his personal number, it was decided he would call us. So the day arrives and our phone rings. With nervous excitement, we answer the phone and talk to… Bret's publicist! We were informed that due to some vocal issues, he was canceling all interviews for the day. Nooooo! After some back and forth, Bret decided he would do exactly one interview that day—with us!

Shockingly, the interview went very well, despite the three of us being in three different locations, using a landline phone with a tiny microphone suctioned to it and connected to a cassette recorder. And right in the middle of the interview, my wife runs past me holding our young son having a bathroom emergency. You never saw that during an MTV interview!

Among other things, he discussed their first video, which pretty much nobody saw, and how the band spent their last $8,000 to shoot the "Talk Dirty to Me" video that jump-started their career. Brett also discussed his love of country music as well as dealing with Juvenile Diabetes. We spoke for about twenty minutes until his throat started hurting and then he wrapped it up. He even passed along the following sage advice before leaving, "If you can write stuff, publishers are out there… every successful artist has 12 million failures until they get to their success."

As this is a book, his advice seems like a good place to wrap this up and get back to the business of trivia. Like, what's Bret's real name? You didn't think it was actually Bret Michaels did you?

https://www.melodic-rock.com/interviews/bretmichaels.html

If you can write stuff, publishers are out there…every successful artist has 12 million failures until they get to their success.

—Bret Michaels

CHAPTER 2
YOU GIVE LOVE A BAD NAME

Names, names, names. This chapter deals with everything pertaining to an artist's name or a band's name. It includes questions about real names, nicknames, former band names and anything else you can think of related to names. If this were a trivia book about '70s television, you'd probably find a question like, "What is Sam, the butcher's last name on *The Brady Bunch?*" It's Franklin, of course. You know, Alice Nelson's boyfriend. That's right, her last name was Nelson. You see, it's going to be easy.

1. "Satch" is the nickname of which axe slinger?
A. Steve Vai
B. Joe Satriani
C. Vivian Campbell
D. Satchel Paige

2. According to Webster, this metal band could be called, "Infectious Disease Found In Cattle and Sheep Which is Transmittable to Humans."
A. Anthrax
B. Biohazard
C. SARS
D. Mad Cow

3. Alsace Lorraine was the original working title of what band?
A. Nightwish
B. Doro
C. Saraya
D. Swiss Lorraine Cheese

4. Before becoming Bonfire in 1985, what were the German rockers originally named?
A. Der Komissar
B. Cacumen
C. Krokus
D. I Need Matches

5. Before Queensrÿche, Kelly Gray and Geoff Tate were formerly members of what band?
A. Mammoth
B. Myst
C. Myth
D. Madonna

6. Before they were Brighton Rock, they were known as what?
A. Brighton
B. Heart Attack
C. Razor
D. The Bee Gees

7. Before they were called Stryper, what were they called?
A. Salvation
B. Roxy Music
C. Roxx Regime
D. Criss Cross

8. What is Bruce Dickinson's first name?
A. Barry
B. Bruce
C. Paul
D. Esmerelda

9. Before they were in Def Leppard, Pete Willis and Rick Savage were both in another lesser known band by what name?
A. Savage
B. Atomic Mass
C. Lion
D. Hearing Impaired Feline

10. Black Sabbath got their name from the title to a novel by what occult writer?
A. Edgar Allen Poe
B. H. P. Lovecraft
C. Dennis Wheatley
D. Dave Barry

11. Dio's muscle-bound devil mascot goes by what name?
A. Eddie
B. Murray
C. Jimmy
D. Bob

12. Faster Pussycat got their name from what?
A. A Groucho Marx flick
B. A James Bond movie
C. A Russ Meyer movie
D. A slow dog

13. From what did Krokus get their name?
A. A movie
B. A bug
C. A flower
D. A space alien

14. How did Britny Fox get their name?
A. A band member's relative
B. Λ cartoon
C. A B-movie from the 1970s
D. Britney Spears

15. Motorhead's front man is known simply as Lemmy, but what is his last name?
A. Kilgore
B. Kilmister
C. Karson
D. Van Halen

16. What is Doro's last name?
A. Posch
B. Porsch
C. Pesch
D. The Explorer

17. Rat Salad nearly became the name of what legendary band?
A. Slade
B. Ratt
C. Van Halen
D. Caesar Salad

18. Rod Morgenstein and Steve Morse were members of what '70s band?

A. 10cc
B. Supertramp
C. The Dixie Dregs
D. Pussycat Dolls

19. Before Queensrÿche, Mike Wilton and Chris DeGarmo were members of what band?

A. Joker
B. Jester
C. Jaguar
D. Jamiroquai

20. Ronnie James Dio was a member of all the following bands EXCEPT...?

A. Orc
B. Vegas Kings
C. Electric Elves
D. Elf

21. Several members of what famous prog metal band used to be members of Cross+Fire and The Mob?

A. Dream Theater
B. Queensrÿche
C. Symphony X
D. Bananas in Pajamas

22. Skid Row's guitarist Dave Sabo is better known by what nickname?

A. The Snake
B. The Shark
C. The Spider
D. Chris Sabo

23. Soft White Underbelly became what popular hard rock band?
A. Blue Öyster Cult
B. Whitesnake
C. Ratt
D. Hard Black Overstomach

24. What is Angus Young's middle name?
A. George
B. Malcolm
C. McKinnon
D. Beef

25. Tesla was formed out of the remnants of what band in 1985?
A. City Slicker
B. Kid Chaos
C. City Kidd
D. Kid Rock

26. The band 415 was also known as what?
A. Fahrenheit
B. The Eric Martin Band
C. FM
D. 400+15

27. The band known as the Edge and then Sneak Preview went on to become famous under what name?
A. Kingdom Come
B. U2
C. King's X
D. King Candy

28. Former GnR drummer's band Suki Jones changed their name to what?
A. Union
B. Samantha 7
C. Adler's Appetite
D. James Earl Jones

29. These glam rockers from Pennsylvania were originally known as Paris before finding stardom.
A. White Lion
B. Poison
C. Warrant
D. The Hiltons

30. What artist is known as "The Red Rocker"?
A. Ted Poley
B. Dave Mustain
C. Sammy Hagar
D. Clifford

31. What band got their name from a group of warriors in Michael Moorcock's "Elric" stories?
A. White Wolf
B. Tygers of Pan Tang
C. Warrior Soul
D. Tiger Woods

32. What is Eddie Van Halen's middle name?
A. Lodewijk
B. Jan
C. Theodore
D. Sally

33. What band got their name when their sister saw it on the back of one of her electrical appliances and made the suggestion?
A. Hotwire
B. AC/DC
C. Electric Boys
D. Hoover Sucks

34. What band was originally named Shooze and then changed their name to The Generators?
A. Tesla
B. The Darkness
C. Kix
D. The Imeldas

35. What did Metallica call themselves when they played a set of Motorhead's greatest hits for Lemmy's 50th birthday party?
A. The Lemings
B. The Lemmys
C. Metallhead
D. Lemmy & the Sunshine Band

36. What did they call themselves before changing their name to Twisted Sister?
A. Twisted Mother
B. Silver Star
C. Big Sister
D. Straight Brother

37. What does the "Y" and "T" stand for in Y&T?
A. Yours & Theirs
B. Yesterday & Tomorrow
C. Yesterday and Today
D. Yams & Turnips

38. What famous metal band was once known as Polka Tulk as well as Earth?

A. Heaven & Earth
B. Iced Earth
C. Black Sabbath
D. The Yankovics

39. What guitar hero once strutted his stuff as a member of a band named Tantrum?

A. Angus Young
B. Joe Perry
C. Vito Bratta
D. Buddy Holly

40. What is Jon Bon Jovi's real surname?

A. Bongiovi
B. Jovi
C. Bon Jovi
D. Bonjourno

41. What is the first name of the scientist that Tesla is named after?

A. Thomas
B. Guglielmo
C. Nikola
D. Liberace

42. What is the name of Jeff Scott Soto's primary hard-rock band from Sweden?

A. Stratovarius
B. Talisman
C. Kamelot
D. ABBA

43. What is Dee Snider's first name?
A. Daryl
B. Darren
C. David
D. Dolores

44. What is the name of the Dangerous Toys clown?
A. Krusty
B. Bill Z. Bub
C. Krazy
D. Boozo the Clown

45. What was the name of the band featuring Bullet Boys drummer Jimmy D'Anda and John Corabi?
A. Zen Lunatic
B. Zen Masters
C. Lunatic Fringe
D. Alabama

46. What was Lemmy's first name at birth?
A. Lemmy
B. Ian
C. Leonard
D. Moonbeam

47. What name did the band Axe go by before becoming Axe?
A. Battle Axe
B. Babyface
C. Sword
D. Axe Not What Your Country Can Do For You

48. What name did Van Halen go by before they called themselves Van Halen?
A. Mammoth
B. Red Ball
C. Atomic Mass
D. Minivan Halen

49. What popular British metal act were originally known as Son of a Bitch?
A. Saxon
B. Bitch
C. Iron Maiden
D. Chicago

50. What rocker is known as "The Motor City Madman"?
A. Ted Nugent
B. Stephen Tyler
C. Paul Stanley
D. Michelin Man

51. What was Dangerous Toys called before becoming Dangerous Toys?
A. Danger
B. Onyx
C. Diamond
D. Hazardous Playthings

52. What was Dream Theater's original name?
A. Dream Big
B. Paradise Theater
C. Majesty
D. Free Popcorn

53. What was Guardian originally called?
A. Fusion
B. Faith
C. Testify
D. The Muppets

54. What is Judas Priest guitarist K. K. Downing's first name?
A. Keith
B. Ken
C. Kyle
D. Lisa

55. What was Harem Scarem named after?
A. 1st Bugs Bunny cartoon
B. Stephen King novel
C. Roger Corman movie
D. Toilet Paper

56. What is Yngwie J. Malmsteen's middle name?
A. Jorn
B. Johann
C. Jay
D. Bob

57. What was the name Lemmy chose for his band before changing it to Motorhead?
A. Bastard
B. Aces
C. Mammoth
D. Gentlemen, Start Your Motorheads

58. What was the name of the band featuring Adrian Smith and Dave Murray before Iron Maiden, which had the album *Black Leather Fantasy*?
A. Irksome
B. Arachnid
C. Urchin
D. Erkel

59. What was the name of the hair metal band featuring brothers Johnny and Joey Gioeli with Journey's Neal Schon on guitar and Deen Castronovo on drums?
A. Hardline
B. Giuffria
C. Gioeli
D. Grape Jelly

60. What is the name of the Playboy Playmate who married Nikki Sixx after he divoriced Brandy Brandt, also a Playmate?
A. Jenna Jameson
B. Donna D'Errico
C. Jenny McCarthy
D. Aunt Bee

61. What was the name of the Bullet Boys album that had a very alternative style as opposed to their traditional hard rock sound?
A. *Acid Monkey*
B. *Arctic Monkeys*
C. *Acid Rock*
D. *Alka Seltzer*

62. What was the name of the KISS tribute band featuring Jaime St. James and Tommy Thayer?
A. Love Gun
B. Cold Gin
C. Black Diamond
D. Kiss My Butt

63. What is the name of the 2022 supergroup featuring Van-Halen's Sammy Hagar and Michael Anthony along with Jason Bonham and Vic Rivera?
A. Van Zeppelin
B. The Circle
C. Chickenfoot
D. The Parallelogram

64. What is Steelheart singer Michael Matijevic's actual first name?
A. Miljenko
B. Marty
C. Malcolm
D. Maude

65. What was the name of the live project, billed as the ultimate tribute to The Who, featuring Gary Cherone, Paul Gilbert, Billy Sheehan, and Mike Portnoy?
A. Who The Funk Are You?
B. Quadrophenia
C. The Amazing Journey
D. The Bird Brains

66. What was the name of the pioneering New Wave of British Heavy Metal group consisting of guitarist Paul Samson, bassist Chris Aylmer, drummer Thunderstick and vocalist Bruce Bruce?
A. Raven
B. Riot
C. Samson
D. 98 Degrees

67. What was the name of the super-group that performed on *Rockline* but never released an album, featuring Sammy Hagar, Neal Schon, Michael Anthony, Joe Satriani, and Deen Castronovo?
A. Soul SirkUS
B. Planet Us
C. Damn Yankees
D. The Wayouts

68. What was UFO originally known as?
A. MSG
B. Hocus Pocus
C. Galaxy
D. Identified Flying Objects

69. Where did Saraya get her name?
A. Her 1st dog's name
B. Her surname
C. Her mother's maiden name
D. Sanjaya

70. What was the names of the twin musicians (drums, keyboards) who played with Yngwie Malmsteen?
A. Anders and Jens Johansson
B. Matt and Gunnar Nelson
C. Liam and Noel Gallagher
D. Frank and Joe Hardy

71. What's the name of the member of Enuff Z'Nuff who gave the band its name?
A. Charles Z. Nuff
B. Chris Z'Nuff
C. Chip Z'Nuff
D. Enough is Enough

72. What is Riki Rachtman's real name?
A. David Alan Rachtman
B. David Lee Rach
C. David Lee Rachman
D. David Allen Coe

73. Which glam band was originally going to be called Christmas?
A. Motley Crüe
B. Cinderella
C. Warrant
D. Easter

74. Who is "The Voice of Rock"?
A. Bruce Dickinson
B. Ronnie James Dio
C. Glenn Hughes
D. Mel Blank

75. Y&T took their name from an album by what band?
A. The Beatles
B. The Who
C. The Rolling Stones
D. The Rutles

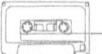

As Night Ranger loudly proclaimed, "You Can Still Rock in America!" And sometimes get tickets, press passes, and meet the band. Could that lead to an interesting story? We have been Night Ranger fans since first hearing "Don't Tell Me You Love Me" back in 1982. Brad Gillis, Jack Blades, and Kelly Keagy played together as members of the pop/funk band Rubicon. The three then formed a band named Stereo, added Alan Fitzgerald and Jeff Watson, then changed their name to Ranger. Trivia alert! Due to a country band named The Rangers, the five rockers changed the name of the band to Night Ranger.

The band has put out thirteen studio albums as of 2021's ATBPO (*And The Band Played On*). We were excited to do a phone interview with guitarist extraordinaire, Brad Gillis, for an online website. Brad was very friendly, open, and a joy to speak with. Additionally, we were told we would get press passes and meet-and-greets. Party on, Wayne! What could go wrong? Well, when we got to will call for the concert, we found we had two meet-and-greet passes, only one press pass, and zero tickets to the show! Oh well, we've bought tickets to hundreds of other concerts so what's one more?

First order of business, the meet-and-greet. As is common, they occur before the show and there are often a lot of people with passes. Therefore, they try to move the people through quickly. The event coordinator made it clear you could get a picture with the band, but you were NOT to ask for autographs because there just wasn't enough time. When it was our turn to meet the band, singer/bassist Jack Blades noticed Ron just happened to be holding a copy of their debut album, certainly not to be autographed or anything. No, that would be against the rules! Of course, the band didn't mind breaking the rules. Jack saw the album, said, "Cool," immediately grabbed it, signed it, and passed it to the rest of the band. The promoter looked rather annoyed, but who cares? We now have an autographed copy of *Dawn Patrol*!

The next step in the adventure was for me to make my way to the press pit to get some pictures. I'm not a professional photographer, so I just showed up with my normal little Sony digital camera. Every single person around me had expensive, professional cameras with these huge wide-angle lenses that looked to be about four feet long. They looked like the paparazzi trying to get a picture of Kim Kardashian's latest boyfriend from a quarter mile away. I stood out like a hot female at a prog rock concert. But I was able to stay in the front row for the first three songs and got some pretty decent shots before heading to the lawn to mingle with the masses. Party on Garth!!

Brad
shredding

Ron and Don Meeting and Greeting
Night Ranger

CHAPTER 3
A.A. MEETING: ARTISTS AND ALBUMS

Some bands have great songs and some bands have great albums. You know the ones, albums that have to be listened to from start to finish. Would you ever start listening to *Dark Side of the Moon* midway through the album? You start at the beginning and let it roll through. Same with *Pet Sounds* and many others like *Close to the Edge* by Yes. And could you really listen to The Dead Milkmen's *Big Lizard in My Backyard* without listening to the whole album? We wouldn't recommend it. But forget about these classic albums, we're here to concentrate on classic metal albums. Just match the albums listed with their correct artist. Easy, right? It's certainly easier than scoring a backstage pass or convincing a hot girl to do cartwheels on your sports car. We have separated the questions into seven sections: General, 21st Century Disks, Debuts, EPs, Solo Efforts, Sophomore Releases, and Live Albums.

GENERAL

As you can see below, we've split this chapter into several sections to organize the questions into logical groupings. However, some simply can't be easily grouped. Either that or we just got too lazy. Either way, below are ten great albums. See if you can match them to their artists.

1. *Blackout*	Aerosmith
2. *Dirty Rotten Filthy Stinking Rich*	Bon Jovi
3. *Heartbreak Station*	Bonham
4. *If You Can't Lick 'Em...Lick 'Em*	Cinderella
5. *New Jersey*	Europe
6. *Permanent Vacation*	Scorpions
7. *Pride*	Ted Nugent
8. *Stay Hungry*	Twisted Sister
9. *The Disregard of Timekeeping*	Warrant
10. *The Final Countdown*	White Lion

Scorpions Still Rocking
Like a Hurricane 2022

21ST CENTURY DISKS

Believe it or not, many of the great hair bands from the '80s didn't stop recording in 1989. Although Grunge did its best to destroy the popularity of this music, it by no means killed it. It just pushed it back underground where it came from.

Many of these bands continue to record new music and tour to this very day. Iron Maiden recently released *Senjutsu* and the Scorpions just released *Rock Believer*. Both are excellent. Granted, a lot of the albums released by these classic bands in the twenty-first century haven't even come close to reaching the popularity of the ones they released in the '80s, but that doesn't mean they're not just as good or even better. We just have to find out for ourselves instead of relying on rock radio or Music-less Television.

I have a feeling some of these are going to be a little difficult, but maybe you'll discover that one of your favorite bands has a new album out and you'll run out and buy it. If so, please remember to send us a finders fee. We take cash, checks, credit cards, and Chuck E. Cheese tokens.

1. *Back To The Rhythm*	Danger Danger
2. *Between the Valley of the Ultra Pussy*	Dio
3. *Ordinary Man*	Faster Pussycat
4. *Lightning Strikes Again*	Great White
5. *Love Grenade*	House of Lords
6. *Magica*	Dokken
7. *Reborn*	Lillian Axe
8. *The Power & The Myth*	Ozzy Osbourne
9. *The Return of the Great Gildersleeves*	Stryper
10. *Waters Rising*	Ted Nugent

DEBUTS

Whether they released twenty albums or only one, they had to start somewhere. This section lists a number of debut albums and you have to match them to their appropriate artist. Easy, right? After all, everyone knows that *Contraband* was Velvet Revolver's debut album. Or was *Velvet Revolver* Contraband's debut album? And *Rest in Sleaze* HAS to be The Sleeze Beez, right? No? Oh, it's the debut album by twenty-first century Swedish sleaze rockers Crashdïet? Oh, the confusion! This is harder than it looks! Oh well, there's only ten questions, might as well get started...

1. *Breaking the Chains*	Bonfire
2. *Don't Touch The Light*	Cinderella
3. *Leather Boys with Electric Toyz*	Dokken
4. *Lonesome Crow*	King Kobra
5. *Look What the Cat Dragged In*	Motley Crüe
6. *Night Songs*	Poison
7. *Ready To Strike*	Pretty Boy Floyd
8. *Too Fast for Love*	Scorpions
9. *Under The Blade*	Twisted Sister
10. *Wild Cat*	Tygers of Pan Tang

Meeting George
Lynch and Lynch Mob

EPs

Sometimes, bands release albums with only a few songs as opposed to the traditional full-length LP. These are called EPs, which stands for "Extended Play." Now, we're not sure how an album with only four or five songs is considered "extended," but what do we know? Maybe we'll start referring to certain smaller body parts as extended to make them sound larger. Like toes. I have extended toes. My toes are extending nicely. I have extremely long, erect, throbbing, pulsating, extending toes. Wait! What??

1. *74 Jailbreak*
2. *A Change of Seasons*
3. *A Tale of Sex, Designer Drugs, and the Death of Rock N Roll*
4. *Believe*
5. *Caution*
6. *Name Your Poison*
7. *Power Love*
8. *Rainmaker*
9. *Relativity*
10. *The Yellow & Black Attack*

Barren Cross
Dream Theater
Impellitteri
Iron Maiden
Lion
Little Caesar
Odin
Pretty Boy Floyd
Stryper
AC/DC

Watching and Meeting Stryper

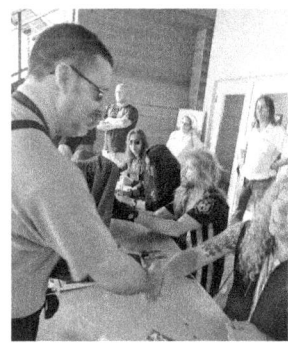

SOLO EFFORTS

Time to go solo. No, we don't mean flying without a co-pilot or anything to do with self-love. We're talking about solo albums.

For some reason, a lot of musicians like to break away from their bands and do their own thing. We don't have a problem with that if the solo stuff doesn't sound exactly like their band; otherwise, why bother? Many people have tried it, some with good results and some, well, not so much.

David Lee Roth had quite a bit of success when he released his little EP with "California Girls," but once he got a taste of not having to split the profits with three other band members, well, it didn't exactly bode well for him after his first few solo albums now did it? On the other hand, you get people like Ozzy Osbourne who was successful in Black Sabbath but also struck out on his own. What ever happened to that guy?

1. A Fine Pink Mist	Bret Michaels
2. Angel Down	Bruce Dickinson
3. Capricorn	Don Dokken
4. Collateral Damage	Jake E. Lee
5. Exposed	Joe Lynn Turner
6. View To a Thrill	Stephen Pearcy
7. Songs of Life	Mike Tramp
8. Tattooed Millionaire	Sabastian Bach
9. The Usual Suspects	Ted Poley
10. Up From The Ashes	Vince Neil

SOPHOMORE RELEASES

Bands that are lucky enough to release a second album either seem to get extremely popular or fall apart. The "sophomore slump" certainly applies to many hard rock bands. Fortunately, most of them fared pretty well. Some did so well that they released tons of albums, making it hard to remember which one came second.

Can anyone honestly remember what the second album by The Beatles or the Beach Boys was? What about AC/DC or Aerosmith? See what I mean? What about Celine Dion? Barry Manilow? Sorry, getting carried away again.

As usual, some of these will probably be easier than others. One thing is certain, many bands get quite creative with the names they choose for their second albums. Others just state the obvious like *Van Halen II* or 707's *The Second Album*. Let's see how well you do with the ten albums we've chosen.

1. *7800° Fahrenheit*	Poison
2. *Break Like The Wind*	Bon Jovi
3. *Cocked and Loaded*	Faster Pussycat
4. *The Great Radio Controversy*	Hurricane
5. *Menace to Sobriety*	L.A. Guns
6. *Over The Edge*	Tesla
7. *Strength in Numbers*	Spinal Tap
8. *Tangled in Reins*	Steelheart
9. *Open Up and Say… Ahh!*	Tyketto
10. *Wake Me When It's Over*	Ugly Kid Joe

LIVE ALBUMS

As anyone who loves rock and roll knows, the best way to experience this music is live. You can't just listen to KISS, you have to experience KISS. Ron made this same argument to his wife once after having seen them about seven times. He finally convinced her to go with him to see them at an outdoor amphitheater. It had nothing to do with him wanting a designated driver. Definitely not. Although the intense thunderstorm that rolled in at the beginning of their set left them scrambling for cover underneath the tiny entrance archway with hundreds of other sweaty fans was a bit of a nuisance, his wife pulled up the straps of her ten-inch platform boots and vowed to make the best of it. That was until some drunk fool accidentally dropped a full jumbo beer on her head. Despite what some shampoo commercials may tell you, a woman does NOT like beer in her hair. Was it really an accident? Would you intentionally throw away a large, full cup of cold draft beer that costs the equivalent of the Gross National Product of a small nation? Exactly!

1. Alive II	Barren Cross
2. Beast from the East	Dangerous Toys
3. Fire and Gasoline	Deep Purple
4. Hotter Than Hell Live!	Dokken
5. Intensities in 10 Cities	Iron Maiden
6. Live After Death	Judas Priest
7. Live At The Roxy - Wake Up Bitch	KISS
8. Made in Japan	Krokus
9. Unleashed in the East	Pretty Boy Floyd
10. Vitamins and Crash Helmets Tour-Live Greatest Hits	Ted Nugent

BANG YOUR HEAD

Quiet Riot burst onto the music scene in 1983 like a hurricane making landfall. The band went from being unknown to topping the charts almost overnight. Their first two big hits were, "Bang your Head (Metal Health)" and "Cum on Feel the Noize," which was a cover song by the British glam rock band Slade. With the help of radio airplay and heavy rotation on MTV, the album *Metal Health* climbed to number one on the Billboard charts. It has gone on to sell over 10 million albums worldwide.

The band was popular enough to acquire the opening slot at the famous 1983 US Festival for the metal day. The classic lineup consisted of singer Kevin Debrow, guitarist Carlos Cavazo, bassist Rudy Sarzo, and drummer Frankie Banali.

Most people think of Quiet Riot as an overnight sensation, which is partially true. Yes, they entered the mainstream and had great success right away; however, the band had been a staple on the L.A. rock scene for almost a decade before hitting it big. In fact, they released two albums in the late '70s, but they were only released in Japan. Here's another fun fact: the original guitar player was legendary Ozzy Osbourne guitarist Randy Rhodes, who played on their first two releases before leaving to join Ozzy's band. Quiet Riot's last charting single in the US came from their 1984 album *Condition Critical*, with yet another Slade cover called "Mama Weer All Crazee Now." Since that album, Quiet Riot has gone on to record ten more studio albums. The latest being 2019's *Hollywood Cowboys*.

Sadly, both Kevin Dubrow and Frankie Banali have passed away and, of course, Randy met an untimely fate after recording only two records with Ozzy. It was Frankie's wishes that the band continue after his passing, so the band embarked on a 2022 tour with the possibility of recording a new album. The current band features Rudy Sarzo, longtime guitarist Alex Grossi, singer Jizzy Pearl, and drummer Johnny Kelly.

We have been lucky to see Quiet Riot in concert numerous times. We've been fans ever since we first heard "Metal Health" blast from our stereo speakers. It was the heaviest song we'd ever heard. The song was so energizing that our high school soccer team cranked it up (on a classic '80s boom box, of course) on the bus before every away game. Along with seeing them in concert, we've also met them several times.

One time, Quiet Riot were touring with several other bands and after their set, they were signing autographs. Don happened to be wearing a colorful KISS farewell tour t-shirt, from their first of many farewells, when Frankie Banali, who was signing autographs, looked up at him and said, "Hey, cool shirt!" It was kind of funny since it wasn't a Quiet Riot shirt! Frankie was very friendly and conversational.

We had another interesting encounter with the band when they played a small local club. After a great performance by the band, we were hanging out after the show as the bouncers were clearing people out of the establishment. Our buddy, Chip, who came with us to the show ran up to us and said, "Hey, I want you to meet a friend of mine." We turned around and his "friend" turned out to be none other than Kevin Dubrow! We chatted for a while and were surprised he was hanging around so long after the gig. Turns out, the band couldn't leave because some idiot's car was blocking their tour bus. We're not going to say whose car it was, but we will say it looked a lot like the car driven by one of the authors of this book.

CHAPTER 4
ANIMAL MAGNETISM

We know. When you think about heavy metal music and the word "animal," you immediately think of that great, romantic song by W.A.S.P. Go ahead and say it. Just yell out the song title. You know you want to. Unless of course you're in a quiet library or the coffee bar at your local bookstore or basically anywhere in public. You might just get yourself escorted right out. Now if you're reading this in a strip bar between dances and you yell out the title, you just might get a date. And if you don't know what song we're talking about, you'll probably find this chapter to be a bit difficult. But if you really don't know, just do an internet search on the song "Animal" by W.A.S.P. to find out the full title of the song. Then you'll understand. Actually, this chapter has nothing to do with that song, but it was a fun intro to write. This chapter is all about bands with animal names, songs with animal names, condiments with animal names, dancers with animal names, animals with animal names…

1. "Monkey Bars" was a popular tune by what Canadian band?
A. Coney Hatch
B. Triumph
C. April Wine
D. The Monkees

2. "Monkey On Your Back" and "Fantasy" were two rock hits for what artist in the mid '80s?
A. Bryan Adams
B. Aldo Nova
C. Bon Jovi
D. Madonna

3. "Of Wolf and Man" is a howling good song by which band?
A. Metallica
B. Metal Church
C. Melodica
D. Manowart

4. "Powerlove" was a song and video for what animalistic metal band?
A. Lion
B. White Lion
C. Whitesnake
D. Alvin and the Chipmunks

5. "Rat Salad" is an instrumental song from which legendary metal band?
A. Judas Priest
B. Ratt
C. Black Sabbath
D. Iron Chef

6. *Animal House* was the debut solo album by which metal singer's band?
A. Rob Halford
B. Udo Dirkschneider
C. Phil Lewis
D. Bluto!

7. What 2007 band featured Ugly Kid Joe's singer and members of Godsmack?
A. Manimal
B. Another Animal
C. Animal Logic
D. Ugly Kid Rock

8. Before becoming a member of Ratt, bass player Juan Croucier was formerly a member of what other famous metal band?
A. Dokken
B. Poison
C. Cinderella
D. The Bay City Rollers

9. Before they were known as Ratt, they were called what?
A. Rat
B. Vermin
C. Mickey Ratt
D. Mouseketeers

10. Clock is a side project by which member of Def Leppard?
A. Vivian Campbell
B. Phil Collen
C. Joe Elliot
D. Screech Powers

11. "Dance of the Dogs" appears on which album featuring guitarist George Lynch?
A. *Sacred Groove*
B. *Wicked Sensation*
C. *Breaking the Chains*
D. *Curious George*

12. "Eagles Fly", written and performed by Sammy Hagar, is co-produced by Sammy and what other artist?
A. Eddie Van Halen
B. Ted Templeman
C. Keith Olsen
D. Don Henley

13. The band 40 Cycle Hum features drummer Francis Ruiz, formerly of what fishy metal band?
A. Shark Island
B. Great White
C. Reel Big Fish
D. Sharknado

14. Great White founder and guitarist Mark Kendall teamed up with vocalist Todd Griffin on what blues rock project?
A. Train Station
B. Great Blue
C. Bus Station
D. Radio Station

15. Guitarist Jeff LeBar played in the band Whitefoxx before replacing Michael Kelly Smith in what big-hair band?
A. Cinderella
B. Britny Fox
C. Tesla
D. Cindy Brady

16. Helloween sang an ode to what heavy metal vermin?
A. Hamster
B. Guinea Pig
C. Rat
D. Blue Green Algae

17. What band had *Animal Magnetism*?
A. Scorpions
B. Tarantulas
C. Krokus
D. Snoop Lion

18. Marq Torien, Mick Sweda, and Lonnie Vincent all left King Kobra to form what band?
A. Whitesnake
B. Bulletboys
C. Blue Murder
D. Depeche Mode

19. Name Def Leppard's guitar player who appeared on early albums such as High 'N' Dry but was replaced by current member Phil Collen.
A. Pete Wagoner
B. Pete Willis
C. Pete Williams
D. Pete Rose

20. Name the beautiful actress who was briefly married to Whitesnake's lead singer and starred in some of their videos.
A. Tawny Kitaen
B. Pamela Anderson
C. Heather Locklear
D. Bobby Dall

21. Name the short instrumental song which "Bringin' On The Heartbreak" leads immediately into on Def Leppard's album *High 'N' Dry*.
A. "Switch"
B. "Switch 625"
C. "Eruption 235"
D. "Fahrenheit 451"

22. The song "Night Wolf" by what German metal band starts off, "I walk the city streets, and I'm looking for some tushie"?
A. Accept
B. Bonfire
C. Krokus
D. Teen Wolf

23. *Prepared to Strike*, released in 1984 by what short-lived glam metal band from Kansas featured guitarist Jacky Foxx?
A. King Kobra
B. Vyper
C. Python
D. Worm

24. "Rattlesnake Shake" is the title of three different songs by three different hard rock bands. Which band did not record a song by this title?
A. Aerosmith
B. Motley Crüe
C. Dokken
D. Skid Row

25. Shark Island was born out of the ashes of what band?
A. Great White
B. Hammerhead
C. The Sharks
D. We're going to need a bigger boat

26. Sleeze Beez members Andrew Elt and Don van Spall went on to form what rock band?
A. The Sun
B. The Moon
C. The Stars
D. Moon the Stars

27. What animalistic rock group sang the song "Who's Behind the Door"?
A. White Lion
B. Zebra
C. Lion
D. The Hampsters

28. "Rock Believer" is the debut single and title track to what predatory arachnid's 2022 album?
A. Black Widow
B. Scorpions
C. Tarantula
D. Peter Parker

29. The metal band Viper, formed in 1985, came from which country?
A. Brazil
B. Australia
C. Germany
D. Dodge City

30. The musicians Snake, Piggy, Blacky, and Away make up what French-speaking thrash metal band?
A. Anthrax
B. Voivod
C. Gwar
D. The T-Birds

31. Ohio meets Japan to release *Kicked & Klawed* by what feline band?
A. Kitty
B. Cats in Boots
C. Radioactive Cats
D. Puss in Boots

32. Beowulf vocalist Tony Lee Wise was also the vocalist for what Florida-based power metal band in the early '90s?
A. Damn Cheetah
B. Wildkatz
C. Tyger Tyger
D. Hippopotamus

33. What animalistic metal band had the song "Calling"?
A. Leatherwolf
B. White Lion
C. White Wolf
D. Pussycat Dolls

34. Sleeze Beez members Jan Koster and Chriz van Jaarsveld went on to form what band?
A. Airport
B. Mach III
C. Jetland
D. Jetsons

35. What artist sings the oddly titled instrumental, "Aardvark in a VW Smoking a Cigar"?
A. Dweezil Zappa
B. Michael Schenker
C. Steve Vai
D. Arthur

36. What band did Jake E. Lee join after leaving Mickey Ratt ?
A. Ozzy
B. Badlands
C. Rough Cutt
D. The Osmonds

37. What band did Stryper alumni Oz Fox and Tim Gaines create in the '90s, whose debut album was called *He's Not Dead*?
A. Sin City
B. SIN
C. Sin Dizzy
D. Slayer

38. What band did the "Dirty Dog" and was in "Heavy Metal Love"?
A. House of Lords
B. Hurricane
C. Helix
D. Lassie

39. What band did Tony Harnell sing with before joining Norwegian band TNT?
A. White Lion
B. Whitefoxx
C. Yellowcard
D. Yellow Snow

40. What band did Vito Bratta play with before finding major success in White Lion?
A. Dream Theater
B. Dreamer
C. Street of Dreams
D. Dream Weaver

41. What band featuring Shark Island's guitarist did Vivian Campbell join in 1990 after becoming so impressed with them while producing their first CD?
A. Def Leppard
B. Dio
C. Riverdogs
D. Hansen

42. What band wanted to "Take The Dog Off The Chain"?
A. AC/DC
B. KISS
C. Babylon A.D.
D. Backstreet Boyz

43. What does W.A.S.P. stand for in the metal world?
A. We Are Sexual Perverts
B. White Anglo Saxon Protestants
C. We Are Sexual Princes
D. Wiggles Are Supremely Popular

44. What famous metal singer sang the theme for the character "Big the Cat" on Sega's "Sonic the Hedgehog" and sang the first stage of the sequel "Sonic 2"?
A. Ted Poley
B. Ronnie James Dio
C. Danny Vaughn
D. Cher

45. What guitarist played in Whitefoxx before gaining greater success in another Philadelphia act Heaven's Edge?
A. Reggie Smith
B. Reggie Wu
C. Reggie Young
D. Reggie Jackson

46. What is the name of Def Leppard's drummer who continued as their sole drummer despite losing his arm in a tragic auto accident?
A. Steve Clark
B. Rick Allen
C. Rick Savage
D. Max Headroom

47. What is the name of the band that briefly included Jake E. Lee as well as Michael Guy from Shark Island and Tony Franklin?
A. Babylon A.D.
B. Bourgeois Pigs
C. Tempest
D. The Wonder Pets

48. What is the name of the female rapper on the Slash's Snakepit tune "Mean Bone"?
A. Raya Beam
B. Queen Latifah
C. Left Eye Lopez
D. Jim Beam

49. What legendary country artist co-wrote the Def Leppard tune "Nine Lives" from their 2008 album?
A. Toby Keith
B. Kenny Chesney
C. Tim McGraw
D. Grandpa Jones

50. Name the popular actress whose legs graced the cover of Ratt's independently released EP *Ratt*.
A. Carmen Elektra
B. Christie Brinkley
C. Tawny Kitaen
D. Lou Christie

51. What legendary guitarist played in the band Shark Frenzy before achieving superstar success?
A. Joe Perry
B. Richie Sambora
C. Joe Satriani
D. Jo' Momma

52. What legendary vocalist appears as a guest vocalist on The Lizards 2006 release *Against All Odds*?
A. Steve Perry
B. Joe Lynn Turner
C. Glenn Hughes
D. Dean Martin

53. What metal band did Whitesnake guitarist John Sykes form with drum legend Carmine Appice?
A. Black and Blue
B. Black Sabbath
C. Blue Murder
D. Black Betty Bam-A-Lam (Whoa)

54. What metal band put out the oddly titled *Pink Bubbles Go Ape*?
A. Anthrax
B. Helloween
C. Baton Rouge
D. King Kong

55. What metal vocalist originally sang on the Scorpions' classic album *Blackout* while Klaus Meine recovered from throat surgery?
A. Michael Kiske
B. Ronnie James Dio
C. Don Dokken
D. Andy Griffith

 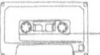

56. What reptilian '80s metal band was formed by Rod Stewart's legendary drummer Carmine Appice?
A. King Kobra
B. Snakepit
C. Whitesnake
D. Boy George and the Karma Chameleons

57. What singer has a song called "I'm Alive (That Was the Day My Dead Pet Returned to Save My Life)," from his 1982 album?
A. Michael Kiske
B. Alice Cooper
C. Paul Stanley
D. Mini Cooper

58. What was Great White's follow-up record to their platinum selling 1987 album *Once Bitten...*?
A. *Twice Bitten*
B. *Bitten Again*
C. *...Twice Shy*
D. *Bite Me*

59. What was the name of Aldo Nova's album featuring the anti-drug song "Monkey On Your Back"?
A. *Monkey On Your Back*
B. *Subject*
C. *Say No*
D. *Monkeys Smokin' Crack*

60. What was the name of Ratt's successful producer who also produced Warrant and Kix?
A. Robert John "Mutt" Lange
B. Bruce Fairborn
C. Beau Hill
D. Bruce Jenner

61. What was the name of the famous nightclub owned by Riki Rachtman and Faster Pussycat's Taime Downe?
A. Cathouse Club
B. The Whiskey
C. The Viper Room
D. McDonalds

62. What was the name of Hollywood legend Milton Berle's nephew who signed Ratt initially to his Time Coast Records label?
A. Marshal Berle
B. Michael Berle
C. Martin Berle
D. Marshal Amp

63. What was the spin-off Tygers of Pan Tang band formed by former members Robb Weir and Jess Cox?
A. Tyger Tyger
B. Tygers of Pan Am
C. Black Tiger
D. Tygers of Peter Pan

64. When Ratt was playing the L.A. circuit, what type of music did they advertise as playing?
A. Hard Rock
B. Heavy Metal
C. Fashion Rock
D. Hillbilly

65. *When the Blackbird Sings* is the 1991 album by what band?
A. Nexx
B. Heart
C. Saraya
D. The Beatles

66. Which band has an album called *Black Tiger*?
A. White Lion
B. Bombay Black
C. Y&T
D. The Festrunk Brothers

67. Which band sang the song "Fast as a Shark" from their 1982 *Restless and Wild* which is one of the first true thrash metal tunes ever recorded?
A. Great White
B. Accept
C. Anthrax
D. Big Guppy

68. Which member of Ratt produced the debut Lillian Axe album?
A. Robbin Crosby
B. Stephen Pearcy
C. Bobbie Blotzer
D. Mickey Mouse

69. Which member of Winger also played for Dokken and Whitesnake?
A. Kip Winger
B. Rudy Sarzo
C. Reb Beach
D. Kip Dokken

70. Which song from Def Leppard's hugely successful *Pyromania* album launched them into superstardom?
A. "Photograph"
B. "Rock of Ages"
C. "Foolin'"
D. "Groovy Grubworm"

71. Whitesnake's huge 1987 hit "Here I Go Again" originally appeared on their earlier 1981 album by what name?
A. *Saints and Sinners*
B. *Sinners and Saints*
C. *Denim and Leather*
D. *Robert Plant is Me*

72. Who replaced Stephen Pearcy as lead singer of Ratt?
A. Jizzy Pearl
B. John Corabi
C. Warren DeMartini
D. Jizzy Up The Girl

73. Who sang the song "Beat To Death Like a Dog"?
A. Rhino Bucket
B. Dirty Looks
C. Kix
D. Garfield

74. Who sings backup on the Ratt tune "Heads I Win (Tails You Lose)" from their 1994 *Detonator* album?
A. Stephen Tyler
B. Jon Bon Jovi
C. Michael Anthony
D. Paris Hilton

75. Who was fired from the British rock band Hawkwind in the mid 1970's?
A. Justin Hawkins
B. Fast Eddie Clarke
C. Lemmy
D. Larry Byrd

ROCK YOU LIKE A HURRICANE

The Scorpions are one of Germany's greatest exports, right up there with Beethoven and bock beer. It's hard to believe they've been together nearly sixty years, forming in 1965. To put that into perspective, that was three years *before* Sebastian Bach was even born! Even more unbelievable, they're still performing live and releasing new music! Their debut album *Lonesome Dove* was released way back in 1972 when men last walked on the moon. Their most recent release is 2022's impressive *Rock Believer* which they supported with a month-long Vegas residency and world tour. Unlike many of their contemporaries, they have remained fairly stable, with three of their five members having been in the band for nearly forty-five years. And those who have left have a pedigree as great as those who have stayed. Former members include such rock luminaries as Michael Schenker, Uli Jon Roth, and Herman Rarebell. Even their most recent addition, drummer Mikkey Dee, came from the British legend Motorhead.

We've been fortunate enough to see them live a few times, including the great Monsters of Rock tour where they played alongside rock legends Metallica and Van Halen. We can safely say the Scorpions have always been, and continue to be, one of the greatest live acts to ever strap on electric guitars and rock a stage. If you've never seen them, get one of their live albums to get a taste of what you've been missing. We prefer *World Wide Live*.

Although all the shows we've seen have been memorable, one that was particularly memorable wasn't even supposed to happen. Back in 1991, my brother and I were bartending at an outdoor amphitheater during the summer, still do as a matter of fact. I had requested working the backstage bar that summer. Today, it's a full-size VIP bar, but back then it was only open during intermission. I requested it because I knew that I'd get to hear the show and then once I finished, I could watch the rest of it. Imagine my surprise when I show up at my bar, only to be told that my services weren't needed because they needed extra storage space due to having three bands. Great White and Aldo Nova were opening that concert. Fearing that I might get reassigned to commandeer an ice cream cart, I slowly made my way back to the office. Since the show had already started, they told me to clock out. I got to watch Aldo Nova play songs from his new *Blood on the Bricks* album along with his other hits, followed by Great White and then the mighty Scorpions. The show was amazing as expected.

After the show, I was visiting a friend who guarded the gate to the backstage area when she asked me if I wanted to come in. You see, they decided to hold the Scorpion's after show meet-and-greet in my little ol' bar area. I naturally said yes, and she quickly whisked me through the gate. All was good except for one little problem. The people waiting to meet the band all had huge backstage passes stuck to the front of their clothes! Not having the required credentials, I conveniently turned around every time I saw one of their security personnel approaching. It worked. Within a few minutes, several members of the band walked out and started mingling. They came out and I distinctly remember meeting singer Klause Meine and thinking, how could such a small guy have such a big voice? To cap off a perfect night, I even got a few of their autographs, which over the impending decades I have managed to lose. But I really did meet them. No, really!

CHAPTER 5
UNDER THE COVERS

Cover songs are songs which were originally recorded by one artist and later recorded by another artist. Many times the cover song becomes much more popular than the original version. Do you know who originally recorded "Hound Dog?" It wasn't Elvis. It was a woman named Big Mama Thornton.

Other times contemporary artists attempt to put their spin on a truly classic song and you're left wondering, "What were they thinking?!" In fact, one big hair artist attempted a remake of Jimi Hendrix's "Purple Haze" on his debut album. Any idea who it was?

In this section, a cover song is listed along with either the original artist or the metal artist who did the remake. Your job is to match them up. Be prepared, you may know who originally sang Mötley Crüe's, "Smokin' in the Boy's Room," but do you know who originally sang Tesla's, "Little Suzi" or Hardline's, "Hot Cherie"? We've separated the questions into two sections: Cover Songs and Cover Albums.

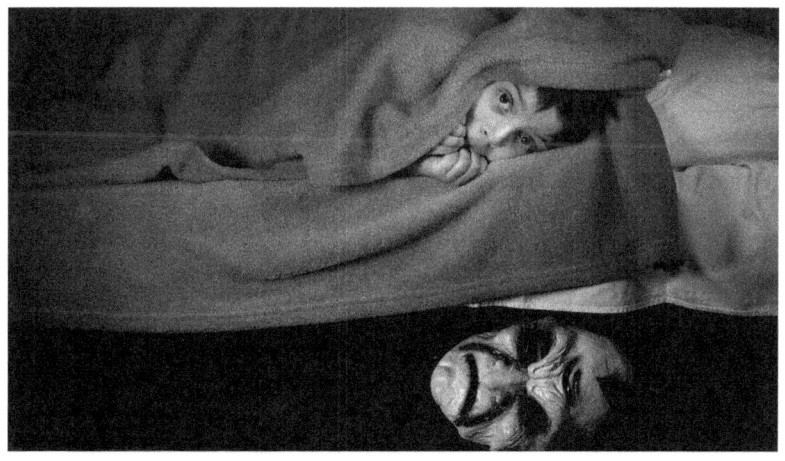

COVER SONGS

Sometimes artists simply run out of ideas and other times they just want to pay homage to a great song. Metal artists certainly did their part in covering previous songs, some ended up being far superior to the originals and others, well, let's just say they should've left well enough alone. We're happy to say that none of them turned out quite as poorly as little Cindy Brady singing her lispy version of "Frosty the Snowman," but some came close. And yes, we have Cindy's version on CD and, yes, it's truly horrible. Don't believe us? Then by all means, look for it on the internet and give it a listen yourself. After finishing our book, of course. But beware, we can not be held responsible for any damage inflicted upon your ear drums. In the meantime, we have collected forty of the best classic metal cover tunes we could find. See which songs you can match with their original and cover artist.

ROCK HARD

1. "That's Life" – David Lee Roth
2. "Helter Skelter" – Motley Crüe
3. "I Can't Explain" – The Who
4. "Hard Luck Woman" – KISS
5. "The Real Me" – The Who
6. "Cat's in the Cradle" – Harry Chapin
7. "Radar Love" – Golden Earring
8. "Crash Course in Brain Surgery" – Metallica
9. "Wild Thing" – Sam Kinison
10. "Don't Be Cruel" – Elvis Presley
11. "Ballroom Blitz" – Sweet
12. "Do Ya" – E.L.O.
13. "Signs" – Tesla
14. "Anarchy in the U.K." – Sex Pistols
15. "Smokin' In The Boys Room"
    – Mötley Crüe

Scorpions
White Lion
Mötley Crüe
W.A.S.P.
Frank Sinatra
Krokus
The Beatles
Cheap Trick
Ace Frehley
Ugly Kid Joe
Brownsville Station
Budgie
The Troggs
Five Man Electrical
Band
Garth Brooks

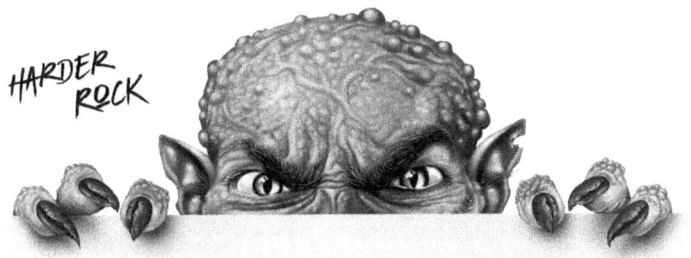

HARDER ROCK

1. "Rock Candy" – Montrose
2. "Cover of the Rolling Stone" – Dr. Hook
3. "Once Bitten, Twice Shy" – Great White
4. "Bloodstone" – Judas Priest
5. "All The Way From Memphis" – Mott the Hoople
6. "The Green Manalishi" – Judas Priest
7. "Shining Star" – Earth, Wind & Fire
8. "Piece of my Heart" – Janis Joplin
9. "Your Mama Don't Dance" – Poison
10. "Stayed Awake All Night" – Krokus
11. "Leader of the Pack" – Twisted Sister
12. "Parasite" – KISS
13. "Because the Night" – Patti Smith
14. "You're So Vain" – Carly Simon
15. "Let The Music Do The Talking" – Aerosmith

Fleetwood Mac
Faster Pussycat
Stryper
Anthrax
Ian Hunter
Stratovarius
Poison
Shangri-Las
Rough Cutt
Contraband
Keel
Loggins and Messina
Bachman-Turner Overdrive
The Joe Perry Project
Bulletboys

LITTLE BLUE PILL

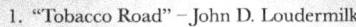

1. "Tobacco Road" – John D. Loudermilk
2. "A Whiter Shade of Pale" – Procol Harum
3. "Hot Cherie" – Danny Spanos
4. "Antisocial" – Antrhax
5. "Love is All Around (Mary Tyler Moore show theme)" – Sonny Curtis
6. "Little Suzi" – Tesla
7. "New York Groove" – Ace Frehley
8. "God Gave Rock and Roll to You" – Argent
9. "Since You've Been Gone" – Russ Ballard
10. "Walking the Dog" – Aerosmith/Ratt

PhD
David Lee Roth
Joan Jett & the Blackhearts
Trust
Hardline

Impellitteri
Rufus Thomas
KISS
Hello
HSAS

COVER ALBUMS

Sometimes bands aren't simply satisfied covering one or two songs, they end up doing an entire covers album. For the most part, they're pretty crappy. It's just a way for artists to make a quick buck. Of course, they'll tell you that they're paying tribute to their influences and heroes. Think about it, they don't have to write the songs but simply play them, record them, and sell them. Not a bad deal. It's the same reason bands release Greatest Hits packages (Aerosmith is soon to release their Greatest Hits vol. 259). Many times, artists do the same thing with Christmas albums. Of course, that's not usually a good option for metal bands. Can you imagine a band like Twisted Sister doing a Christmas album? Oh, wait a minute… Below are ten covers albums. See if you can match them to their artists.

1. *$5.98 EP: Garage Days Re-revisited*
2. *Feedback*
3. *Metal Jukebox*
4. *Poison'd*
5. *Real to Reel*
6. *Take Cover*
7. *The Hitlist*
8. *The Spaghetti Incident?*
9. *Under Cover*
10. *Yeah!*

Joan Jett
Helloween
Guns N' Roses
Def Leppard
Metallica
Ozzy
Poison
Queensrÿche
Rush
Tesla

EVERYBODY WANTS SOME VAN HALEN

In 1978, brothers Alex and Edward Van Halen, along with Michael Anthony and David Lee Roth, burst onto the music scene. Rock-'n'-roll was never the same! Their debut album is considered one of the greatest rock debuts of all time. Not surprising considering it features the Kink's cover "You Really got Me," radio staple "Jamie's Cryin'," concert favorite, "Ain't Talkin' 'Bout Love," and the song that introduced the world to Eddie's famous tapping, "Eruption." The album sold over 10 million copies in the U.S. This classic lineup of the band went on to record five more albums, all of which went multi-platinum. Their sixth album, *1984*, also sold over 10 million copies and features the band's only number one single in the U.S., the infectious, keyboard-heavy song "Jump."

By this time, Eddie Van Halen was often regarded as one of the greatest guitar players of all time, right up there with Jimi Hendrix. He was always pushing the boundaries of the instrument. From his tapping, to the effects/volume knob manipulation on "Cathedral" to the electric drill used on "Poundcake," Eddie was an experimental guitar genius. Frank Zappa famously thanked him for reinventing the electric guitar. Eddie gave some guitar lessons to Frank's son Dweezil and even produced his first single.

The band was also blessed to have David Lee Roth who ranks as one of the most charismatic front men of all time, right up there with Mick Jagger and Freddie Mercury. After highly successful albums, it was a shock when he left the band to pursue a solo career. Could the band survive? Obviously, yes! Legendary Montrose singer and successful solo artist Sammy Hagar joined the band right after riding the success of his monster hit "I Can't Drive 55." All four VH studio albums with Sammy out front went platinum. Their first album *5150* was their first to reach #1 on the Billboard charts. The next three albums reached #1 as well, spawning numerous hit songs. The band was also nominated for two Grammy awards and won for Best Hard Rock Performance with Vocal for their *For Unlawful Carnal Knowledge* album.

Van Halen changed singers one more time with Extreme vocalist Gary Cherone. They released one album, 1998's *Van Halen III* which didn't reach the success of the Sammy albums but still went Gold and had one hit song, "Without You." We saw the supporting tour and enjoyed it because Gary sang a lot more Roth-era songs than Sammy did, and Michael Anthony even sang lead vocals on a song. Cherone was, and is, a great singer, just not a great fit for Van Halen. They released their final album *A Different Kind of Truth* in 2012, featuring the return of Roth on vocals and Eddie's son Wolfgang on bass. The album sold well, received positive reviews, and produced a successful tour. Sadly, Eddie passed away from cancer in 2020. Another trivia alert–starting with their *For Unlawful Carnal Knowledge* tour, and then on following tours, Night Ranger's Alan Fitzgerald played keyboards offstage, so Eddie could focus on playing the guitar.

We've seen Van Halen numerous times and were lucky to see all lineups of the band with all three singers. In fact their *1984* tour was the second concert we attended. It was so loud it took a full minute into the opening song before we realized they were even playing "Unchained"! It was a great show.

David was at his rock star best, Michael was rocking his Jack Daniels' bass, Alex commanded his mammoth 4-bass drum kit (with flaming gong), and Eddie played like the icon he is. We went to the show with a group of school friends. One of them smuggled in some weed. Some fans in front of us offered him a trade, their beer for his joint. He agreed. Within a few short minutes a security guard shined a flashlight on the guys who immediately dropped it. The guard asked what they were smoking, so they picked up an old cigarette butt which satisfied the guard. Unfortunately, they had dropped their treasure onto the soggy, sticky, beer-covered floor. They turned around and asked for their beer back. Sorry fellows, a trade's a trade!

Although it's sad Eddie passed, and the band has disbanded, there is some good news for fans. Wolfgang released a successful album in 2021 called *Mammoth WVH* in which he wrote all songs, sang, and played all instruments. The song "Distance" was nominated for a Grammy award. In 2022, Sammy Hagar and the Circle, featuring Michael Anthony, released a new album, *Crazy Times*, and went on tour. We attended one of the shows and along with Hagar, Montrose, and The Circle songs, it also featured a lot of great Van Halen songs. The Van Halen legacy lives on!

VH Merch
Including T-Shirt &
Ticket Stub from
our 2nd concert

CHAPTER 6
NOT!

This chapter is all about knots… slip knots, butterfly knots, overhand knots, square knots, Prusik knots, Knott's Berry Farm, Knots Landing, Don Knotts……NOT! The key to this chapter is for you to know so much about music that you NOT only know a lot about the topic in question, but you also know what does NOT fit. Like which is NOT a vegetable? A: Carrots, B: Peas, C: Tomatoes, D: Broccoli. Don't worry, nobody else knows either. But, we digress. This is NOT the time to put down the book and give up. You can do eeet!

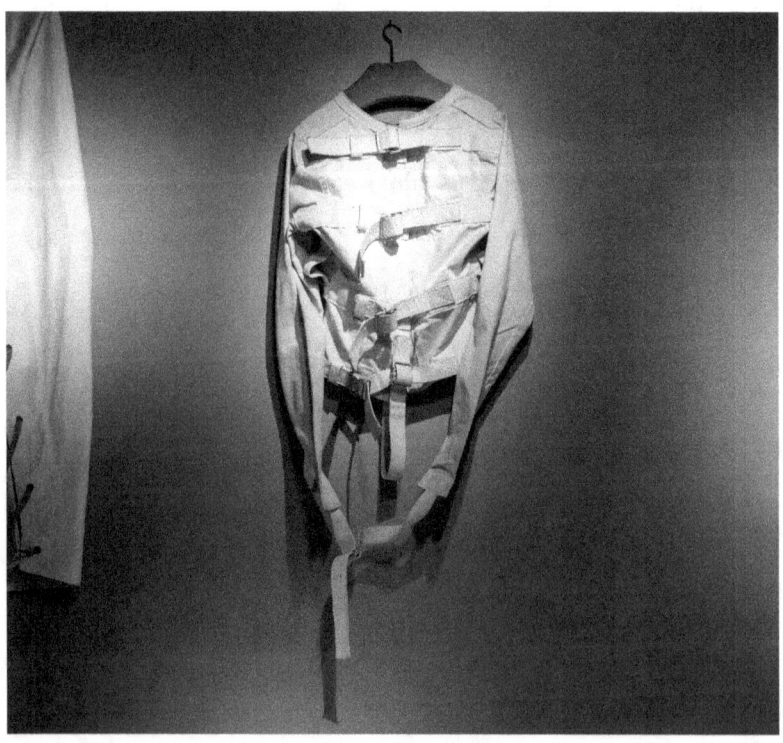

1. What is NOT the name of one of Spinal Tap's ficticious albums?
A. *Intravenus de Milo*
B. *Metaphysical Graffiti*
C. *The Sun Never Sweats*
D. *Smell the Glove*

2. Billy Sheehan played in all of the following bands except...
A. Talas
B. Last Autumn's Dream
C. Niacin
D. Mr. Big

3. Jason Newsted has NOT played in which band?
A. Echobrain
B. Voivod
C. Megadeth
D. Flotsam and Jetsam

4. John Corabi was in all of the following bands except…
A. Motley Crüe
B. Ratt
C. Union
D. The Angels

5. Vivian Campbell played in all of the following bands except…
A. Dio
B. Def Leppard
C. Motley Crüe
D. Whitesnake

6. What artist has Vinny Appice NOT worked with?
A. Spade Thomas
B. Black Sabbath
C. John Lennon
D. Ozzy

7. What band did drummer Carmine Appice NOT play in?
A. Rod Stewart
B. Deep Purple
C. Blue Murder
D. King Kobra

8. What band did Freddy Curci NOT sing with?
A. Tyketto
B. Sheriff
C. Alias
D. Zion

9. What band did Jeff Scott Soto NOT sing with?
A. Talisman
B. UFO
C. Journey
D. Axel Rudi Pell

10. What band has bassist Chuck Wright NOT played with?
A. Impelliteri
B. Quiet Riot
C. Warrant
D. House of Lords

11. What band has bassist Marco Mendoza NOT played in?...
A. Thin Lizzy
B. Quiet Riot
C. Whitesnake
D. Dolores O'Riordan of The Cranberries

12. What band has bassist Pete Way NOT been a member of?
A. Fastway
B. Waysted
C. UFO
D. Iron Maiden

13. What band has bassist Robbie Crane NOT played with?
A. Crane
B. Ratt
C. Vince Neil
D. Saints of the Underground

14. What band has Cozy Powell NOT played drums with?
A. Rainbow
B. The Raspberries
C. The Brian May Band
D. Michael Schenker Group

15. What band has drummer Jimmy DeGrasso NOT played with?
A. Y&T
B. Megadeth
C. Tora Tora
D. Suicidal Tendencies

16. What band has drummer Pat Torpey NOT played with?
A. Impelliteri
B. Mr. Big
C. Ted Nugent
D. Whitesnake

17. What band has drummer Simon Wright NOT played in?
A. AC/DC
B. Rhino Bucket
C. Ronnie James Dio
D. Blanc Faces

18. What band has drummer Steven Adler NOT played in?
A. Velvet Revolver
B. Guns 'N Roses
C. Adler's Appetite
D. Bulletboys

19. What band has Eric Singer NOT played in?
A. KISS
B. Black Sabbath
C. Badlands
D. Aerosmith

20. What band has Gary Cherone NOT been a member of?
A. Babylon A.D.
B. Extreme
C. Van Halen
D. Tribe of Judah

21. What band has Graham Bonnet NOT sung with?
A. Black Sabbath
B. Impelliteri
C. MSG
D. Rainbow

22. What band has Gregg Giuffria NOT played with?
A. Bombay Black
B. Giuffria
C. Angel
D. House of Lords

23. What band has guitarist Lanny Cordola NOT been in?
A. House of Lords
B. Mondo Cane
C. Giuffria
D. Firehouse

24. What band has guitarist Steve Brown NOT played in?
A. Trixter
B. 40 Ft. Ringo
C. Warrant
D. Stereo Fallout

25. What band has Jake E. Lee NOT played in?
A. Red Dragon Cartel
B. Badlands
C. Mickey Ratt
D. Winter

26. What band has James Christian NOT sung for?
A. Jasper Wrath
B. House of Lords
C. Eyes
D. Jasmine

27. Which of the following Black Sabbath albums did NOT feature Ronnie James Dio?
A. *Sabotage*
B. *Heaven and Hell*
C. *Mob Rules*
D. *Dehumanizer*

28. What band has Jeff Pilson NOT played in?
A. Waysted
B. Dokken
C. Foreigner
D. Dio

29. What band has Jizzy Pearl NOT sung with?
A. Love/Hate
B. Dokken
C. Ratt
D. L.A. Guns

30. What band has Joe Lynn Turner NOT sung with?
A. Sunstorm
B. Mother's Army
C. Rainbow
D. Black Sabbath

31. What band has John Sykes NOT played in?
A. Thin Lizzy
B. Tygers of Pan Tang
C. Tesla
D. Whitesnake

32. What band has Paul Shortino NOT sung in?
A. Rough Cutt
B. Badd Boys
C. Quiet Riot
D. The Cult

33. What band has Ray Gillen NOT sung in?
A. Black Sabbath
B. Badlands
C. Rondinelli
D. Deep Purple

34. What band has Reb Beach NOT played in?
A. Beach Boys
B. Winger
C. Whitesnake
D. Dokken

35. What band has Richie Kotzen NOT played with?
A. Poison
B. Forty Deuce
C. Mr. Big
D. Richie & The Students

36. What band has Rob Halford NOT been the lead singer in?
A. Judas Priest
B. Halford
C. Fight
D. D'Priest

37. What band has Rob Rock NOT sung in?
A. Metallica
B. Impellitteri
C. Axel Rudi Pell
D. Joshua

38. What band has Rudy Sarzo NOT played in?
A. Quiet Riot
B. Rainbow
C. Dio
D. Whitesnake

39. What band has singer Danny Vaughn NOT played in?
A. Waysted
B. Vandenburg
C. Circus Circus
D. Tyketto

40. What band has singer Paul DiAnno NOT sung in?
A. Iron Maiden
B. Battlezone
C. Jaguar
D. Killers

41. What band has Steve Grimmett NOT played in?
A. Grim Reaper
B. Guardian
C. Onslaught
D. Lionsheart

42. What band has Ted Poley NOT sung with?
A. Danger Danger
B. Melodica
C. Fastway
D. Bone Machine

43. What band has Tommy Aldridge NOT played drums with?
A. Ozzy Osbourne
B. Quiet Riot
C. Whitesnake
D. Motorhead

44. What band has Jason McMaster NOT sung in?
A. Kreator
B. Dangerous Toys
C. Broken Teeth
D. Ignitor

45. What band has vocalist Jorn Lande NOT sung with?
A. Ark
B. Allen/Lande
C. Masterplan
D. Lande's End

46. What is NOT an Ozzy Osbourne Live album?
A. *Ozzmosis*
B. *Speak of the Devil*
C. *Tribute*
D. *Just Say Ozzy*

47. What is NOT the name of an Aerosmith greatest hits album?
A. *Gems*
B. *Young Lust*
C. *Pandora's Toys*
D. *Rocks*

48. What is NOT the name of an Iron Maiden live album?
A. *Live After Death*
B. *A Real Live One*
C. *Maiden China*
D. *A Real Dead One*

 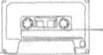

49. What is the only Quiet Riot album NOT to feature Kevin DuBrow?
A. *Condition Critical*
B. *Quiet Riot II*
C. *Quiet Riot (1988)*
D. *QRIII*

50. What singer has NOT fronted the band Impelliteri?
A. Rob Rock
B. Graham Bonnet
C. Eric Martin
D. Curtis Skelton

51. What was NOT one of the reported methods that Spinal Tap's drummers perished?
A. Gardening Accicent
B. Listening to Disco
C. Choked on Vomit
D. Spontaneous Human Combustion

52. Which band did Kelly Hansen NOT sing in?
A. Hurricane
B. Blue Murder
C. Unruly Child
D. Perfect World

53. Which band did Mark Free NOT play in?
A. FREE
B. Unruly Child
C. Signal
D. King Kobra

54. Which Bon Jovi album did NOT go to #1?
A. *Lost Highway*
B. *New Jersey*
C. *Crush*
D. *Slippery When Wet*

55. Which ex-Guns 'N Roses member was NOT a member of Velvet Revolver
A. Slash
B. Matt Sorum
C. Steven Adler
D. Duff McKagan

56. Which guitarist was NOT a member of the original G3 lineup?
A. Kenny Wayne Shepherd
B. Joe Satriani
C. Eric Johnson
D. Steve Vai

57. Which of the following artists are NOT a member of Supernova?
A. Izzy Stradlin
B. Tommy Lee
C. Jason Newsted
D. Gilby Clarke

58. Which of the following bands did Kelly Keeling NOT play with?
A. Blue Murder
B. King Kobra
C. Baton Rouge
D. Vanilla Fudge

59. Which of the following bands did NOT feature guitar-great Magnus Karlsson?
A. Last Tribe
B. Allen/Lande
C. Starbreaker
D. TNT

60. Which of the following bands did NOT lose the first ever Grammy Award for Best Rock/Heavy Metal band?
A. Motorhead
B. Metallica
C. AC/DC
D. Jane's Addiction

61. Which of the following bands has NOT released a live album from Budokan?
A. Ozzy Osbourne
B. Van Halen
C. Cheap Trick
D. Dream Theater

62. Which of the following bands were NOT honored as part of VH-1's first ever Rock Honors in 2006?
A. KISS
B. Def Leppard
C. Judas Priest
D. Ozzy Osbourne

63. Which of the following is NOT a Dio album?
A. *Magician*
B. *Angry Machines*
C. *Strange Highways*
D. *Sacred Heart*

64. Which of the following is NOT a KISS album?
A. *Rock and Roll Over*
B. *Dressed to Kill*
C. *Destroyer*
D. *Renegade*

65. Which of these are NOT considered concept albums?
A. *Operation Mindcrime*
B. *Powerslave*
C. *Lovemetal*
D. *Keeper of the Seven Keys, Pt. 1*

66. Who has NOT been a singer for Krokus?
A. Marc Storace
B. Mandy Meyer
C. Carl Sentence
D. Tommy Kiefer

67. Who has NOT been a singer for L.A. Guns?
A. Ralph Saenz
B. Jizzy Pearl
C. Kevin Chalfant
D. Chris Van Dahl

68. Who has NOT been one of Vince Neil's wives?
A. Jules Asner
B. Sharise Ruddell
C. Beth Lynn
D. Heidi Mark

69. Who has NOT done a version of "God Gave Rock and Roll To You"?
A. KISS
B. Stryper
C. Argent
D. Petra

70. Who has NOT starred in a reality TV show?
A. C.C. Deville
B. Bret Michaels
C. Vince Neil
D. Bobby Dall

71. Who was NOT a bass player for The Runaways?
A. Cherry Johnson
B. Jackie Fox
C. Micki Steele
D. Vicki Blue

72. Who was NOT a featured vocalist on Herman Rarebell's 1985 solo album?
A. Don Dokken
B. Jack Russell
C. John Waite
D. Charlie Huhn

73. Who was NOT a founding member of Badlands?
A. Jake E. Lee
B. Ray Gillen
C. Ian Gillan
D. Eric Singer

74. Who was NOT a member of ESP?
A. Eric Singer
B. Bob Kulick
C. John Corabi
D. Karl Cochran

75. Who was NOT a member of VH-1's 2006 Supergroup?
A. Sebastian Bach
B. Ted Nugent
C. John Bonham
D. Evan Seinfeld

Chilling with Y&T's
Dave Meniketti

TRAIN KEPT A ROLLING

Just another band out of Boston. We know, those are lyrics from a different band. But stay with us. When thinking of great rock and roll cities, you often think of places Like New York, L.A., or Seattle. But Boston gave us bands like, well, Boston, but also The Cars, The Pixies, The Lemonheads, American Hi-Fi and one of the biggest, most successful rock bands of all time–a little band called Aerosmith!

Aerosmith first hit it big in the 1970s creating songs that are still played on classic rock radio today. Some of their legendary songs like "Sweet Emotion" and "Walk This Way" came from 1975's *Toys in the Attic*. The next year they released *Rocks* with classics like "Back in the Saddle" and "Last Child." All four of these songs are found on their iconic 1980 Greatest Hits album with the red cover. As teens in the mid '80s, we used to crank up that cassette all the time. It was great, but at the time it seemed like Aerosmith's best days were behind them. Their later albums didn't have the hits, the band members weren't getting along, and they seemed relegated to just a great classic rock band from the past, like Led Zeppelin, Foghat, or the Doors. Boy, were we wrong!

They had an unprecedented resurgence in the 1980s. Their 1987 album *Permanent Vacation* gave them three popular singles, "Dude Looks Like a Lady," "Angel," and "Rag Doll". Their songs were all over the radio and MTV. This is also when they re-recorded "Walk This Way" with Run-D.M.C., which helped break down race barriers and exposed both rock and rap to different audiences. The band were now popular for a whole new generation. Their next album, *Pump* in 1989 was even more successful. It had four hits, including "Love in an Elevator" and "Janie's Got a Gun" and went multi-platinum. They carried their success into the '90s with *Get a Grip* which had even bigger sales and reached number one on the charts.

Their longevity, popularity, resilience, and influence are truly amazing. They've amassed numerous AMA, Billboard, and MTV awards to name a few. They've even won four Grammy awards and have been nominated fourteen times. Impressively, except for a few short years since forming in 1970, the band has always consisted of the same five guys: Steven Tyler, Joe Perry, Brad Whitford, Joey Kramer, and Tom Hamilton. They are now cultural icons. Steven Tyler has been a judge on American Idol, and the band even appeared in a legendary "Wane's World" SNL sketch. They have appeared in, and had their music used in movies and video games, including *Guitar Hero: Aerosmith*. They even have their own Disney World ride, the Rock 'N' Roller Coaster! And as of the 2022 writing of this book, they are still on tour, fifty-two years after forming!

Naturally, we have an interesting personal Aerosmith story. In the early '90s they rolled into town with Jackyl. Although Ron had to work, I went with a group of friends and was excited because the seats were only about fifteen rows back from the stage. When arriving at the seats, there were a few big, burly, biker dudes already occupying them. Being hospitable, it was agreed they could remain in our seats for the opener but would have to leave once Aerosmith started. Everyone agreed, and all was good. Or so it seemed. Once Aerosmith hit the stage, surprise, surprise, the Neanderthals changed their minds and decided not to leave. Calm, rational discussion was attempted but to no avail. Now of course we should've just grabbed an usher and waited to have them ejected. But being young, dumb, and feeling bulletproof, a few of the guys (and girls) got mouthy. Then some pushing began. Then fists started flying. Temporarily losing my mind, I grabbed one of the huge dudes in a headlock and yelled, "BREAK IT UP!" Presumably thinking I was security he stopped fighting. Which is fortunate because he probably would've thrown me back several rows, which is exactly what happened to my friend. It wasn't pretty. The bikers finally took off but, unfortunately, so did we when we took our friend to First Aid and later, to the hospital. He ended up being all right, but we missed what was, by all accounts, a great concert. At least it generated a good story. Who knows, maybe it'll end up in a book someday!

Ron with Derek St. Holmes and
Aerosmith's Brad Whitford

CHAPTER 7
MATH SUCKS

Believe it or not, there really is a song called "Math Sucks." It's done by the legendary Jimmy Buffett as somewhat of a joke. It's not exactly "Margaritaville," but it strikes a universal chord nonetheless. Regardless of how you feel about math, we have decided to add our own little math section to this book. Now before you start hyperventilating and having flashbacks to Algebra class (or Geometry class, or Intro to Simple Fractions, or Addition for Dumb-Asses) don't fret, this math test will be much more entertaining. We promise. So grab your calculator, your slide rule, your pocket protector, and your taped up glasses. Class is about to begin. If a train kept a rollin' all night long from Chicago, and another *Night Train* leaves *New York Groove* at the same time…

1. Alice Cooper + Dixie Dregs
A. Warrant
B. Winger
C. Whitesnake
D. Dixie Chicks

2. Alice in Chains + Jellyfish + Guns 'N Roses
A. Adler's Appetite
B. Slash's Snakepit
C. Ju Ju Hounds
D. Run in Your Hoses

3. Axl Rose + Tracii Guns
A. Brides of Destruction
B. Hollywood Rose
C. Gun 'N Roses
D. Culture Club

4. Badlands + House of Lords + The Firm + Shark Island
A. Blitzkrieg
B. Proletariat
C. Bourgeois Pigs
D. Wilbur the Pig

5. Bang Tango + Faster Pussycat + Bullet Boys
A. Cock Fight
B. Big Cock
C. Cocked & Loaded
D. Joe Cocker

6. Black Sabbath + Ozzy
A. Bad Finger
B. Badlands
C. Bad Company
D. Bad Mamma Jamma

7. Blind Vengeance + Minotaur
A. Blind Minotaur
B. Harem Scarem
C. RUSH
D. One Eyed Snake

8. Candice Night + Ritchie Blackmore
A. Blackmore's Night
B. Black Night
C. Candie Nightmore
D. Deepthroat Purple

9. Carl Dixon + Dave Ketchum + Steve Shelski + Andy Curran
A. Danger Danger
B. Angel
C. Coney Hatch
D. Mr. Big Lots

10. Cinderella + Ratt + Sea Hags
A. Arcade
B. Dokken
C. Poison
D. Popeye

11. Contagious+Brave New World+Ten
A. XYZ
B. Metal Church
C. Vaughn
D. The Partridge Family

12. Dangerous Toys + Dirty Looks
A. Raven
B. Danger Danger
C. Broken Teeth
D. That's So Raven

13. Dream Theater + Fates Warning
A. CSI
B. OSI
C. FBI
D. IOU

14. Elf + Deep Purple
A. Roxy
B. Rainbow
C. Whiskey
D. Studio 54

15. Eric Martin + Jack Blades
A. Damn Yankees
B. TMG
C. TMZ
D. Dang Rebels

16. Europe + Fair Warning + Mikael Erlandsson
A. White Wolf
B. Danger Danger
C. Last Autumn's Dream
D. Oingo Boingo

17. Mythology + Rare Breed
A. Dio
B. Black Swan
C. Black Sabbath
D. Medium Rare Breed

18. Fastway + Krokus + The Untouchables + The Meanies
A. Gotthard
B. Bad English
C. Katmandu
D. The Fast, Mean, Untouchable Kroki

 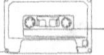

19. Free + AC/DC + Led Zeppelin
A. The Law
B. The Firm
C. The Lawfirm
D. The John Grishams

20. Iced Earth + Blind Guardian
A. Demons & Wizards
B. Dungeons & Dragons
C. Denim & Leather
D. Captain & Tenille

21. KISS + Def Leppard + Quiet Riot + Motley Crue + Van Halen + Alice Cooper
A. The Dudes of Rock
B. The Dudes of Hazard
C. The Dudes of Wrath
D. The Grapes of Wrath

22. Guns 'N Roses + Quiet Riot + White Lion + W.A.S.P.
A. Velvet Revolver
B. Slash's Snakepit
C. Hookers and Blow
D. Quiet Guns 'N White WASPs

23. Guns 'N Roses + Ratt + Faster Pussycat
A. Slash's Snakepit
B. Velvet Revolver
C. Adler's Appetite
D. Guns 'N Pussies

24. Guns 'N Roses + Stone Temple Pilots
A. Slash's Snakepit
B. Velvet Revolver
C. Adler's Appetite
D. The Stone Roses

25. Guns N' Roses + Girl + W.A.S.P.
A. L.A. Guns
B. Adler's Appetite
C. Velvet Revolver
D. Guns N' Wasps

26. Hager + Schon + Aaronson + Shrieve
A. SHAS
B. HSAS
C. HASS
D. ASS

27. Heart + Sheriff
A. Alias
B. Firehouse
C. Vixen
D. Deputy Fife

28. House of Lords + Alice Cooper + Ratt + Warrant
A. Saint & Sinners
B. Saints of the Underground
C. Saints of Leon
D. Minnesota Saints

29. Iron Maiden + The Cult
A. The Untouchables
B. Iron Cult
C. Touch
D. Iron City Beer

30. Michael Sweet + Marco Mendoza + Joel Hoekstra +
Tommy Aldridge + Nathan James
A. Legend
B. Iconic
C. Ironic
D. Pentatonix

31. Joe Lynn Turner + Phil Soussan + Carlos Cavazo + Vinny Appice
A. Gypsy Rose
B. Kamelot
C. Big Noize
D. The Osmonds

32. John Sykes + Carmine Appice + Tony Franklin
A. Black 'N' Blue
B. Badlands
C. Blue Murder
D. Blues Clues

33. Jack Blades + Deen Castronova + Doug Aldridge
A. Saints & Sinners
B. Revolution Saints
C. Revolution Calling
D. Switchblade Casanova

34. Kansas + Steelhouse Lane
A. Seventh Key
B. Asia
C. Steelheart
D. Bowling Lane

35. King Kobra + Hurricane
A. Blue Murder
B. Unruly Child
C. Stryper
D. Rainy Snake

36. King's X + Dream Theater + Dixie Dregs
A. Tiger
B. Alligator
C. Platypus
D. Blue Green Algae

37. KISS + Motley Crüe
A. Union
B. Vinnie Vincent Invasion
C. Asia
D. Men in Makeup

38. Love/Hate (Jizzy Pearl) + L.A. Guns (Stacey Blades) +
W.A.S.P. (Mike Duda) + The Firm (Chris Slade)
A. Fire Whiskey
B. 80 Proof
C. 100 Proof
D. Kool Aid

39. Mabel + Dreamer + Angel
A. Whiteheart
B. White Lion
C. Whitesnake
D. Dream Angel

40. McCoy + MAYA
A. Savatage
B. Saxon
C. Samson
D. Sally Strouthers

41. Montrose + Journey + Van Halen
A. Alias
B. Damn Yankees
C. Planet Us
D. Van Leunens

42. Motely Crüe + Metallica + Guns 'N Roses
A. Rock Star Supernova
B. Rock Star Supergroup
C. Rock Star Supermen
D. Rock Star Supermarket

43. Motley Crüe + L.A. Guns
A. Brides of Destruction
B. Adler's Appetite
C. Slash's Snakepit
D. L.A. Crüe

44. Motorhead + UFO + Humble Pie
A. Montrose
B. Fastway
C. Triumph
D. Humble Head

45. Nelson + Night Ranger + Slaughter
A. Bad English
B. Damn Yankees
C. Scrap Metal
D. Enya

46. Night Ranger + Rainbow + Journey + Vanilla Fudge
A. Mother's Army
B. Mother's Navy
C. Father's Marine Corp
D. Baby's

47. Ozzy + Dokken + Steelheart + Bonham
A. Dragon
B. Badlands
C. Steel Dragon
D. Puff the Magic Dragon

48. Phil Mogg + Mick Bolton + Pete Way + Andy Parker
A. Fastway
B. UFO
C. M.A.P.P.
D. The Silver Convention

49. MSG + Winger + Dokken + Mr. Big
A. Blackboard Jungle
B. Black Swan
C. Black Dawn
D. None More Black

50. Rainbow + Quiet Riot + Mr. Big
A. Impelliteri
B. Deep Purple
C. Masterplan
D. Mr. Bill

51. Joe Lynn Turner + Pink Cream 69
A. Sunstorm
B. Firestorm
C. Solar Flare
D. The Russells

52. Dokken − Don + Robert Mason
A. Black and Blue
B. Lynch Mob
C. The End Machine
D. The Washing Machine

53. RIOT + Danger Danger + TNT + Blue Oyster Cult/ Rainbow
A. Wonderland
B. Whitesnake
C. Westworld
D. Wonderarma

54. Skid Row + Anthax + Bonham + Damn Yankees + Biohazard
A. Damnocracy
B. Skid Yankees
C. Skid Hazard
D. Skid Marks in Your Pants

55. Steeler + ICON
A. Keel
B. Union
C. Talisman
D. U.S. Steel

56. Styx + Night Ranger + Amboy Dukes
A. Damn Yankees
B. Bad English
C. Asia
D. Dukes of Hazzard

57. Ted Poley + Gerhard Pichler
A. Melodica
B. Acoustica
C. Melody
D. Pee Pee

58. The Blackhearts + Lita Ford + The Bangles
A. Warlock
B. Cherry Bombs
C. The Runaways
D. YWCA

59. The Troggs + Tone Loc + Sam Kinison
A. "Wild One"
B. "Wild Thing"
C. "Wild Katz"
D. "Wild & Crazy Guys"

60. TNT + Last Tribe + Los Angeles Project
A. Last Autumn's Dream
B. Starbreaker
C. Lionheart
D. Parliament Funkadelic

61. TNT/SHY+ MSG + Vox Tempus + The Storm
A. Midnight Blue
B. China Blue
C. Arctic Blue
D. Blue's Clues

62. Tony MacAlpine + Tommy Aldridge + Rob Rock + Rudi Sarzo
A. M.A.R.S.
B. R.A.P.S.
C. A.R.M.S.
D. Sweaty Armpits

63. Tracii Guns + Joe LeSte + Chip Z'Nuff
A. A1A
B. Route 66
C. US 66
D. Heinz 57

64. Billy Sheehan + Mike Portnoy + Richie Kotzen
A. The Reservoir Dogs
B. The Winery Dogs
C. The Junkyard Dogs
D. The Deputy Dawgs

65. Ty Tabor + Doug Pinnick + Jerry Gaskill
A. Overkill
B. Living Colour
C. King's X
D. Hogan's Heroes

66. Tytan + Steeler
A. White Lion
B. Whiteheart
C. Lion
D. The Pistoleros

67. UFO + AC/DC + Magnum
A. Collateral Damage
B. Damage Control
C. Damage Plan
D. The AC/DC Boys

68. UFO + Heartbreakers + Flying Squad + Wild Horses
A. Blue Murder
B. Fastway
C. Waysted
D. Moody Blues Clues

69. Van Halen + Red Hot Chili Peppers
A. Switchfoot
B. Chickenfoot
C. Switch
D. Chicken Salad

70. Vanilla Fudge + Detroit Wheels + Amboy Dukes
A. Desert Fox
B. Cactus Juice
C. Cactus
D. Amboy Dukes of Hazzard

71. W.A.S.P. + MSG + Motley Crüe + Guns N' Roses + Ratt
A. The Metal All Stars
B. Metal Madness
C. The Big Ball Stars
D. The Rockettes

72. Winger + Dream Theater + King's X
A. JAM
B. Ram Jam
C. Jelly Jam
D. Jelly Fish

73. Winger + Night Ranger + Whitesnake + King's X
A. The Mob
B. King's Rangers
C. White Ranger
D. Power Ranger

74. Derek Sherinian + Glenn Hughes + Joe Bonamassa + Jason Bonham
A. 21 Guns
B. Black Star Riders
C. Black Country Communion
D. Orange is the New Black

75. Zodiac Mindwarp's Love Reaction + D.O.A.
A. Four Horsemen
B. Third Eye Blind
C. Tall Stories
D. The Groovy Grubworms

Don & Ron Meet
Anvil's Lips

Ron and Anvil's
Robb Reiner

YESTERDAY AND TODAY

Y&T is a legendary hard rock band from Oakland, California. Many people may only know of the band due to their 1985 hit song "Summertime Girls." If so, they really need to do a deeper dive into this amazing band. The band formed in 1972 and was originally named Yesterday and Today, after the 1966 North American album by the Beatles. The band released two albums with that name in the 1970s. Their classic lineup consisted of vocalist/guitarist Dave Meniketti, guitarist Joey Alves, bassist Phil Kennemore, and drummer Leonard Haze.

In the '80s, they simplified their name to Y&T. It was during this time they released their classic albums starting with *Earth-shaker*, *Black Tiger*, and *Mean Streak*. They toured extensively and opened for the biggest acts of the day. Their work ethic, musicianship, and songwriting gained them a loyal following. In concert, they still play many songs from those three albums.

With their 1984 release, *In Rock We Trust*, they finally started getting more mainstream success. The album featured their first big radio hit "Don't stop Runnin'". I recall being a teen and blasting "Lipstick & Leather" and "Life, Life, Life" in our mom's Citation. Nothing says rock and roll like a 1984 Chevy Citation! *In Rock We Trust* turned out to be their best-selling album.

The next year they released *Down for the Count* which featured their most successful single "Summertime Girls." The song was popular on the radio, used in episodes of *Baywatch*, and was all over MTV. Luckily, by this time we were cranking up these songs in our classic 1972 Mustang. In 1987 they released their last charting album and one of our favorites, *Contagious*. Like most metal bands they struggled commercially in the 1990s; however, they still released three solid albums. It then took them thirteen years to release their next, and as of now, last studio album, 2010's *Facemelter*. Not surprisingly, it sounds like classic Y&T!

They've not only inspired many classic metal bands from the '80s, they're also well respected as one of the best live rock bands around. Luckily, my brother and I had a chance to see them perform a few times. The first time we drove over five hours to see them. As expected, they put on an amazing show. We were fortunate to meet and get autographs from Dave and Phil, who sadly passed away not long after.

Unfortunately, Dave is the only current surviving member of the classic lineup. However, he still carries the Y&T torch by touring with new members. We were lucky to see Y&T again in February 2020. It was the last show we saw before the world shut down due to Covid a month later. As usual, the band put on a great, energetic show. They played everything from "Earthshaker" off their first album to "Blind Patriot" from their last album along with all the classic tunes you'd expect.

Ron's teenage son Evan went with us and brought in a vinyl copy of *Down for the Count*. After the show, a roadie noticed the young fan leaning on the stage holding the classic album. He approached him and said, "That's great, would you like me to get the band to sign that?" *Is that a trick question?* The album is now framed and hanging on his wall. A great reminder of a great night.

Ronnie James Dio once stated that Dave Meniketti is one of the most underrated singers on Earth. He happens to be a remarkable guitar player, song writer, and performer. There's a reason they've sold over four million records. As of 2022, Y&T is still touring. If you ever get a chance to see them live, do it! You can thank us later.

CHAPTER 8
CAT MATCH FEVER

Jimi Hendrix was a legendary guitar player, John Bonham was a master of the skins, and Zamfir is the king of the pan flute. Although a few musicians are proficient at multiple instruments, most are known for a particular instrument they've mastered. Rock and rollers are no different. In fact, they've pretty much perfected the art of soloing. This chapter contains three sections, one for drummers, one for guitarists, and one for singers. Time to see if you can match these talented musicians with their respective bands.

DRUMMERS

We'll start with the drummers. It's not because we like them more, but for the highly planned and orchestrated reason that "d" comes alphabetically before "g" and "s." So sit on your throne, grab your stick, and bang your gong. We're talking about drumming here, people. Sheesh!

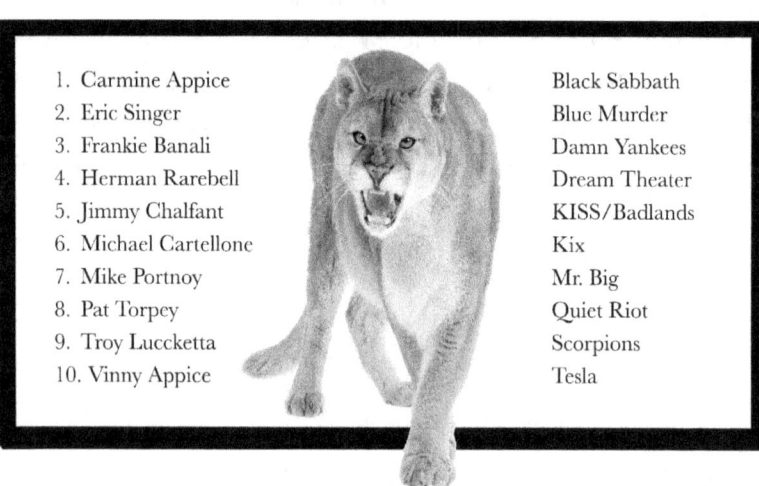

1. Carmine Appice	Black Sabbath
2. Eric Singer	Blue Murder
3. Frankie Banali	Damn Yankees
4. Herman Rarebell	Dream Theater
5. Jimmy Chalfant	KISS/Badlands
6. Michael Cartellone	Kix
7. Mike Portnoy	Mr. Big
8. Pat Torpey	Quiet Riot
9. Troy Luccketta	Scorpions
10. Vinny Appice	Tesla

SINGERS

When it comes to being in a band, it seems that everybody wants to be the lead singer. They get to be center stage and always in the spotlight. In fact, many people's first image of a band is their lead singer. Can you name the members of The Doors, excluding Jim Morrison? It's a little harder isn't it? For the record, it's Ray Manzarek, Robbie Krieger, and John Densmore. Hair bands are no different. Think about Guns 'N' Roses, Poison, and Metallica. Can you visualize their singers? This is another matching section. Simply match the singer with their corresponding band. Okay, who was the lead singer of Culture Club. Just kidding, just kidding...

1. Bob Catley	Autograph
2. Brian Vollmer	Black 'N' Blue
3. Corey Glover	Bullet Boys
4. Danny Vaughn	Cinderella
5. Dave Meniketti	Danger Danger
6. David Glen Eisely	Dangerous Toys
7. David St. Hubbins	Faster Pussycat
8. Doro Pesch	Giuffria
9. Jack Russell	Great White
10. Jaime St. James	Helix
11. James Christian	House of Lords
12. Jason McMaster	Hurricane
13. Jeff Keith	Kix
14. Kelly Hansen	Krokus
15. Marc Storace	L.A. Guns
16. Marq Torien	Living Colour
17. Michael Matijevic	Magnum
18. Michael Sweet	Pretty Boy Floyd
19. Paul Shortino	Quireboys
20. Pete Loran	Rough Cutt
21. Phil Lewis	Spinal Tap
22. Spike	Steelheart
23. Steve Plunkett	Stryper
24. Steve Summers	Tesla
25. Steve Whiteman	TNT
26. Taime Downe	Trixter
27. Ted Poley	Tyketto
28. Tom Keifer	Ugly Kid Joe
29. Tony Harnell	Warlock
30. Whitfield Crane	Y&T

GUITARISTS

Not to be outshined by their drumming and singing counterparts, many guitarists have found stardom in their own right. This is particularly true with respect to rock bands. Generally, the lead guitarist tends to receive most of the attention, but not always. Therefore, we decided to include all types of guitarists in this section, including lead, rhythm, and bass guitarists. Let's see how well you can match the guitarists with their corresponding bands. Grab your amp, your Les Paul, and your hair spray...here we go.

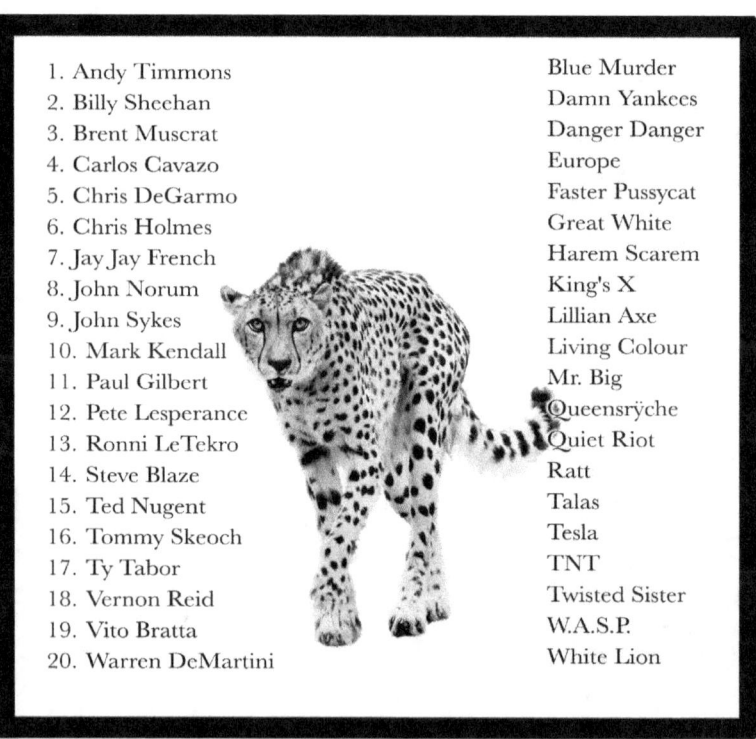

1. Andy Timmons	Blue Murder
2. Billy Sheehan	Damn Yankees
3. Brent Muscrat	Danger Danger
4. Carlos Cavazo	Europe
5. Chris DeGarmo	Faster Pussycat
6. Chris Holmes	Great White
7. Jay Jay French	Harem Scarem
8. John Norum	King's X
9. John Sykes	Lillian Axe
10. Mark Kendall	Living Colour
11. Paul Gilbert	Mr. Big
12. Pete Lesperance	Queensrÿche
13. Ronni LeTekro	Quiet Riot
14. Steve Blaze	Ratt
15. Ted Nugent	Talas
16. Tommy Skeoch	Tesla
17. Ty Tabor	TNT
18. Vernon Reid	Twisted Sister
19. Vito Bratta	W.A.S.P.
20. Warren DeMartini	White Lion

QUEEN OF THE RYCHE

Seattle–home of grunge music. Nirvana, Pearl Jam, Sound-garden, and... Queensrÿche? Yes, they also hail from the Space Needle City, proving the Pacific Northwest is known for more than just grunge, rain, and Bigfoot. Originally known as The Mob, Queensrÿche formed in 1980 as a five piece metal band. Since then, they have released twenty-three albums, consisting of sixteen LPs, including the obligatory covers album, four live albums, two greatest hits compilations and, of course, their introductory, four-song EP. Eleven of them went gold or platinum.

Our friend Skeeter bought the EP on vinyl, and that was our first introduction to the band. We liked it, especially the song that gave them their name, "Queen of the Reich." But it wasn't until their next album that we really became fans, thanks to a couple of other friends, Todd and Dane.

Todd and Dane were in a local rock band with the great name, Gotham City. They were playing at an outdoor party and our friend, Scott, kept requesting "Take Hold of The Flame." They did, and we were hooked. We bought the cassette of their next album, *Rage for Order,* as soon as it came out. It had a more polished sound and even had some videos that hit MTV.

Soon, everyone became fans once the band released their magnum opus, *Operation: Mindcrime.* The concept album raised the bar for heavy metal bands. From this point on, many would refer to their style as "prog metal," along with bands like Dream Theater and Fates Warning.

Later on, we were fortunate enough to see a show featuring

those exact three bands. It was amazing. The success of the album led to a sequel, a live album/DVD, and a name for singer Geoff Tate's new band when they fired him. Their next album, *Empire*, was even more successful, thanks in part to the hit ballad "Silent Lucidity," which exposed them to a whole new audience.

But what goes up must come down. The wheels started slowly coming off shortly thereafter with departures and lawsuits. Original guitarist and chief songwriter Chris De-Garmo left in 1998 with Tate being fired in 2012. Tate went on to release several solo albums and a trilogy of albums under the Operation: Mindcrime moniker. He was replaced by Todd La Torre, who had been fronting Crimson Glory after the tragic death of their singer, Midnight.

In 2017, founding member, drummer Scott Rockenfield took an indefinite break, leaving only two remaining original members. At one point there was even two versions of the band, both of which released albums using the Queensrÿche name, until a court settlement was eventually reached.

We have been fortunate enough to see both the Tate and La Torre versions of the band multiple times. They have never disappointed. We were lucky enough to meet them once thanks to their publicist. Ron volunteered to develop a web site for him and, in return, received backstage passes for their *Operation: Mindcrime II* tour. For several years, the publicist also sent copies of the next few releases such as *Q2K* and *Mindcrime at the Moore*. Not bad considering he never did used the web site!

Fortunately, four decades after releasing their EP, Geoff Tate is still touring and releasing music. The current version of Queensrÿche is touring and releasing music, too. In 2022 they released *Digital Noise Alliance* and continue to release videos from the album and tour. For those of us who love this band, it's a thrill to hear them still cranking out great music. And to those who whine that music isn't as good today as it was in the '80s, point them to this band and tell them to open their minds and crank up some awesome new Queensrÿche!

Meeting House of Lords vocalist James Christian

Chilling with Russell Allen

CHAPTER 9
KISS AND MAKEUP

This chapter is all about Van Halen! Okay, maybe not. But why would we dedicate an entire chapter to just this one band? Well, they have been around for half a century, but so have Aerosmith, AC/DC, and others. The answer is this, KISS was the first rock band we seriously started following when we were young. Aside from *The Monkees Greatest Hits*, our first album was a live KISS album. It was followed shortly thereafter by the newly released solo album by Ace Frehley in 1978 and many others. Although we were never technically in The KISS Army (it's unclear why we weren't, but we're still looking for the recruiting office), we did wear KISS tee-shirts and even had super cool, sparkly KISS belt buckles that we wore to our prestigious sixth grade graduation ceremony, much to the shock and horror of many of our classmates who were secretly envious but sporting the fine suit and tie their parents made them wear.

New Kiss Army Recruits (Alexy, Evan, Ethan, Avery)

1. "I Love It Loud" originally appeared on which KISS album?
A. *Unmasked*
B. *Love Gun*
C. *Creatures of the Night*
D. *Love Gum*

2. "Radioactive" was a song from which KISS member's '78 solo album?
A. Gene Simmons
B. Peter Criss
C. Paul Stanley
D. Peter Cetera

3. After Peter Criss left KISS, what was the name of his official fan club?
A. Criss Army
B. The Cat Club
C. PC3
D. Kiss Off

4. Before joining KISS, name the band Vinnie Vincent played with in the early '80s.
A. Scandal
B. Warrior Soul
C. Warrior
D. The Brady Six

5. Former KISS member Mark St. John teamed up with what other former KISS member after leaving the band?
A. Vinnie Vincent
B. Ace Frehley
C. Peter Criss
D. Donna Summer

6. Guitarist Ace Frehley left KISS and formed his own '80s band by what name?
A. Frehley's Comet
B. Spaceman
C. The Meteors
D. Ace of Bass

7. Immediately after leaving KISS, Mark St. John joined what band featuring ex-Black Sabbath singer David Donato?
A. White Tiger
B. White Lion
C. Whitesnake
D. Edge to Edge Toppings

8. In July 1980, who replaced Peter Criss as the drummer for the legendary rock group KISS?
A. Eric Martin
B. Eric Singer
C. Eric Carr
D. Eric Clapton

9. KISS released the two new studio cuts "Let's Put the X in Sex" and "(You Make Me) Rock Hard" as well as a new version of "Beth" on which of their many greatest hits albums?
A. *Killers*
B. *Smashes, Thrashes and Hits*
C. *Double Platinum*
D. *Let's Put the Al in Alimony*

10. Michael Bolton, yes that Michael Bolton, used to be in what metal band with KISS guitarist Bruce Kulick?
A. Blackjack
B. Black 'N Blue
C. Black Tiger
D. Baa Baa Black Sheep

11. Name the '70s band Gregg Giuffria used to play in, which shared the same label as the legendary KISS.
A. Keel
B. XYZ
C. Angel
D. Village People

12. Name the band Gene Simmons and Paul Stanley were in before they created the legendary KISS.
A. S & M
B. S & S
C. Wicked Lester
D. Smootch

13. Name the band Peter Criss formed with fellow Chelsea member Stan Penridge after leaving KISS.
A. Kittie Kittie
B. The Criss/Penridge Alliance
C. Criss Cat Club
D. Josie & the Pussycats

14. Name the country where Gene Simmons was born.
A. Germany
B. United States
C. Israel
D. Dagoba

15. Name the only KISS album to feature guitarist Mark St. John.
A. *Asylum*
B. *Lick It Up*
C. *Animalize*
D. *KISS and Makeup*

16. Name the exhibitionistic band Eric Carr played with before joining KISS.
A. Flasher
B. Exposed
C. Pervert
D. Don't Look Ethyl

17. Prior to 1998's *Psycho Circus*, what was the last KISS studio album to actually feature all four original members (despite album credits stating otherwise)?
A. *Unmasked*
B. *Dynasty*
C. *Animalize*
D. *Alive MCMLXXXV*

18. Rock legends KISS finally took their makeup off in the early '80s with the release of what album?
A. *Lick it Up*
B. *Unmasked*
C. *Animalize*
D. *Now You Know Why We Wore Makeup*

19. The band Badlands included which KISS drummer?
A. Eric Singer
B. Peter Criss
C. Eric Carr
D. Eric Idle

20. The popular KISS songs "Domino" and "I Just Wanna" are found on which album?
A. *Revenge*
B. *Crazy Nights*
C. *Asylum*
D. *Chinese Checkers*

21. This band's gimmicks included makeup, spitting blood and a drum kit that rotated over the audience. (Hint: The answer is not KISS!)
A. Poison
B. Mötley Crüe
C. Warrant
D. Freddy and the Fishsticks

22. Vinnie Vincent left KISS to form what band?
A. Vinnie Vincent Invasion
B. Slaughter
C. World War III
D. Ace Frehley Invasion

23. What band had the first release on Simmons Records back in 1988?
A. Blue Murder
B. Frehley's Comet
C. House of Lords
D. Air Supply

24. What was the first band to ever play with KISS without makeup?
A. Autograph
B. Black Sabbath
C. Helix
D. Cher

25. What classic KISS tune did Rob Zombie, Gilby Clarke, Scott Ian, Slash, and Tommy Lee play to honor KISS in the first ever VH-1 Rock Honors?
A. "Deuce"
B. "God of Thunder"
C. "Detroit Rock City"
D. "50 Year Old Men in Makeup"

26. What group did you belong to if you were an official fan of the rock band KISS?
A. The KISS Army
B. The KISS Koalition
C. The KISS Klub
D. The Cub Scouts

27. What kind of tatoo does KISS member Paul Stanley have on his upper right arm?
A. A star
B. A rose
C. Puckered lips
D. Mom

28. What number was always associated with original KISS drummer Peter Criss?
A. 13
B. 3
C. 69
D. Pi

29. What record label were KISS on even though it was primarily a disco label?
A. Decca
B. RCA
C. Casablanca
D. Versace

30. What was the first KISS song released to feature Ace on lead vocals?
A. "Rocket Ride"
B. "Shock Me"
C. "Cold Gin"
D. "Hey, That Dude's Wearing My Makeup!"

31. What was the name of A&E's reality television show featuring the family of Gene Simmons?
A. *KISS & Sell*
B. *KISS & Tell*
C. *Family Jewels*
D. *Newleyweds*

32. What was the name of the KISS album that was shelved when the original members reunited but was later released?
A. *Psycho Circus*
B. *Revenge*
C. *Carnival of Souls*
D. *Carnival of Cruises*

33. What was the name of the KISS album where they caught a lot of flack from their fans for dabbling in disco?
A. *Dynasty*
B. *Creatures of the Night*
C. *Hot in the Shade*
D. *Kissco Inferno*

34. What was the name of the least popular KISS album, released in 1981 as a concept album and included the American Symphony Orchestra?
A. *(Music From) The Elder*
B. *Unmasked*
C. *Creatures of the Night*
D. *Smile*

35. What was the name of the new KISS studio album and tour when they first reunited with all four original members?
A. *Psycho Circus*
B. *Carnival of Souls*
C. *Killers*
D. *Barnum and Bailey Circus*

36. What was the name of the newspaper that featured an add for a guitar player for KISS, which was responded to by Ace?
A. *Billboard*
B. *Village Voice*
C. *Rolling Stone*
D. *Mad Magazine*

37. What was the name of the street gang that both Ace Frehley and Blackie Lawless once belonged?
A. The Falcons
B. The Duckies
C. The Dobermans
D. The Lords of Flatbush

38. When KISS guitarist Vinnie Vincent wore makeup with the band, what character was he?
A. Fox
B. Ankh Warrior
C. Cross
D. Vinnie Vincent Price

39. Which classic KISS album was re-issued with a new KISS logo due to concerns about the original logo looking too much like Nazi symbols?
A. *Destroyer*
B. *Double Platinum*
C. *Love Gun*
D. *Alive MMVI*

40. Which former member of KISS formed his own band in 1984?
A. Bruce Kulick
B. Ace Frehley
C. Vinnie Vincent
D. Ace Stradlin

41. Which KISS album featured Peter Criss on the cover even though he didn't write or play on it?
A. *Unmasked*
B. *The Elder*
C. *Revenge*
D. *Criss Cross*

42. Which KISS album originally featured Ace on the cover and then Bruce Kulick on the re-issue even though neither one of them actually played on the album?
A. *Lick It Up*
B. *Creatures of the Night*
C. *Love Gun*
D. *Love Boat*

43. Which KISS guitarist was formerly in The Good Rats and Blackjack before joining the legendary band?
A. Vinnie Vincent
B. Bruce Kulick
C. Mark St. John
D. Ace Simmons

44. Which member of KISS appeared in the tabloids thanks to an imposter who convinced unsuspecting people that he was down on his luck and needed hand-outs?
A. Peter Criss
B. Ace Frehley
C. Vinnie Vincent
D. Peter Brady

45. Which member of KISS did Jaime St. James play in the KISS tribute band he used to be in?
A. Paul Stanley
B. Peter Criss
C. Ace Frehley
D. Peter, Paul & Ace

46. Which member of KISS was electrocuted onstage during a concert in Lakeland, Florida during their *Destroyer* tour?

A. Peter

B. Gene

C. Ace

D. Gumby

47. Which song, co-authored by Paul Stanley, appeared on KISS's *Hot in the Shade* album as well as Ace Frehley's *Trouble Walkin'*?

A. "Rocket Ride"

B. "Do Ya"

C. "Hide Your Heart"

D. "Sticker Shock Me"

48. Who played drums on the KISS album *Unmasked*?

A. Anton Fig

B. Peter Criss

C. Eric Carr

D. Doby Gillis

49. Who played guitar on the KISS album, *Creatures of the Night*, even though he never appeared on the album cover?

A. Bruck Kulick

B. Ace Frehley

C. Vinnie Vincent

D. Michael Jackson

50. Who replaced Ace as the guitarist for KISS after his 2nd departure from the band?

A. Bruce Kulick

B. Tommy Thayer

C. Mark St. John

D. Spade Thomas

YOU WANTED THE BEST

You wanted the best, you got the best, the hottest band in the world–KISS! Ever since we heard those immortal words blasting from the speakers of our stereophonic, quadraphonic, bionic turntable, we were hooked. The year was 1977, and KISS was at the top. The band had recently released *Alive II* (our very first record purchase) and the platinum selling *Love Gun* (which showed up under the Christmas tree that year in the form of an 8-track!) We were in fifth grade and KISS was everywhere. Magazines, TV shows, and, of course, retail stores. In addition to purchasing records, we bought KISS T-shirts, trading cards, and even a box of official KISS makeup so we could look just like our idols. Years later Don pulled off a very good "Peter Criss" for Halloween. You probably saw him on *The Phil Donahue Show*.

Being rabid life-long fans, we longed for the day when we could finally see our favorite band in concert. Our first chance was in the sixth grade when we were offered tickets due to the KISS shirts we were wearing. Our parents weren't as excited about their pre-teen sons attending a rock concert as we were, so we just had to bide our time. And so we did. It was 1985, and we finally got to see them live during their *Animalize* tour. Opening up was a then unknown W.A.S.P., who threatened to kick the ass of a guy who stole a poster they threw out to a fan. He gave it back, not wanting to tangle with a six-and-a-half foot guy with a saw blade in his crotch. When KISS hit the stage, we remembered why we loved them so much. The show was an incredible display of music, smoke, lights, and pyrotechnics. The only downside was not getting to see them in makeup and performing without Peter and Ace. That would be rectified about ten years later. And the price for this amazing experience? Eleven whole dollars.

After that first show, we've seen them many more times, with and without makeup, and with assorted band members. I was even lucky enough to catch my very first guitar pick during their *Asylum* tour. Every show was spectacular. Whether they were breathing fire, spitting blood, flying through the air, playing smoking guitars, igniting explosions, or covering the crowd with confetti, it was always a spectacle. Along with Alice Cooper, they set the bar for live entertainment. Poison, Garth Brooks, and even The Backstreet Boys have implemented portions of KISS live shows. KISS were always trying new things, even incorporating 3-D elements into their *Psycho Circus* tour complete with 3-D glasses. Fans have always showed up to their concerts wearing makeup too, whether the band was wearing makeup or not. Our own kids even wore KISS makeup when they attended their first show. But keep in mind, as Jimmy Buffett warned, "Don't try to describe a KISS concert if you've never seen it." Luckily, we have, so we're suitably qualified!

Space Ace Smokin'
Guitar Solo

CHAPTER 10
S&M: SONGS & MUSICIANS

This is a matching chapter, matching songs to their respective artists. We would elaborate, but it's really pretty straightforward. It's a relatively small chapter, but we thought we'd include it anyway just for fun. We always liked matching questions on tests in school, because the answers were always provided and you got to draw all of those crisscrossing lines on the page and make a general mess of everything. This is no exception. If you've had a few adult beverages while reading this book, this would be a good chapter to tackle now.

CHRISTMAS

Ah the most wonderful time of the year. And some things just go with the Christmas season: Holly and Ivy, Frosty and Rudolph, Mary and Joseph, Christmas music, and heavy metal. Okay so that last one is a bit of a stretch. But it has been done. All you have to do is match the holiday song with the artist who recorded it. I'm sure there may be some alternate artists who have done some of these holiday songs, so don't start complaining. Just match the one's we've given you. It's our book and you'll just have to play along. It will be as fun as dreaming about sugarplums dancing in your head. Does anyone know what a sugarplum is by the way?

1. "Christmas Time Again"
2. "Everyday Should Be Like Christmas"
3. "Father Christmas"
4. "Happy Christmas (War Is Over)"
5. "Heavy Metal Christmas
   (The Twelve Days Of Christmas)"
6. "I Saw Mommy Kissing Santa Claus"
7. "Naughty Naughty Christmas"
8. "Rockin' Around the Christmas Tree"
9. "Run Rudolph Run"
10. "Santa Claus is Coming To Town"
11. "Santa's Back In Town"
12. "Silent Night"
13. "White Christmas"
14. "Winter Wonderland"
15. "Won't Be Home For Xmas"

Bullet Boys
Danger Danger
Dokken
Every Mother's
   Nightmare
Extreme
Faster Pussycat
Firehouse
Gilby Clarke
L.A. Guns
Queensrÿche
Roxx Gang
Stryper
Twisted Sister
Warrant
Winger

Ron and Faster Pussycat's
Chad Smith

INSTRUMENTALS

This next section is essential to our book; in fact, you could say that it's instrumental. Ha! Get it? Instrumental? Wow, such humorously creative brilliance is almost frightening. It's almost Shakespearian. In fact, it's a little known fact William also started his writing career authoring his own music trivia book. He published his masterpiece in the late '80s, 1589 to be exact, which was titled, *Billy's White Wigged Trivia Tome: 1,001 Queries in Which to Clatter Thine Cranium.* We highly recommend it.

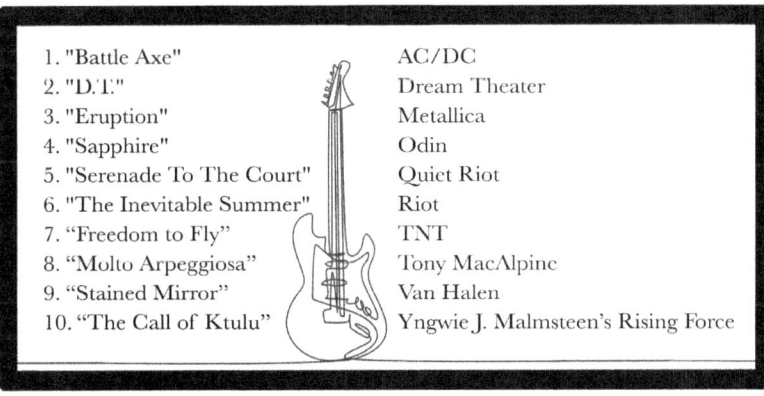

1. "Battle Axe"   AC/DC
2. "D.T."   Dream Theater
3. "Eruption"   Metallica
4. "Sapphire"   Odin
5. "Serenade To The Court"   Quiet Riot
6. "The Inevitable Summer"   Riot
7. "Freedom to Fly"   TNT
8. "Molto Arpeggiosa"   Tony MacAlpine
9. "Stained Mirror"   Van Halen
10. "The Call of Ktulu"   Yngwie J. Malmsteen's Rising Force

Ron, Don and Peter Banging Heads to Joey Allen and Warrant

POWER BALLADS

Nothing says I love you quite like a heavy metal power ballad. For good or bad, a lot of bands in the '80s and early '90s recorded at least one power ballad. It became a formula for success. On the plus side, a lot of the ballads are actually quite good. They also introduced bands to a whole new demographic–females! Sure, rock bands always had groupies, but now you had women who actually liked the songs and bought the albums and concert tickets. On the negative side, some of these good, hard rocking bands only achieved commercial success due to that one ballad. Some of them are probably still in therapy to deal with it. Have fun with this matching section and try to remember if you fell in love while listening to any of these songs. Okay, maybe a lot of people didn't fall in love necessarily, but they sure got sweaty in the back seat of their Camaros to these songs!

1. "Don't Know What You Got (Till It's Gone)"   Blue Murder
2. "Headed for a Heartbreak"   Cinderella
3. "Heaven"   Faster Pussycat
4. "Is This Love"   Kix
5. "When The Children Cry"   L.A. Guns
6. "Bad For Each Other"   Motley Crüe
7. "Don't Close Your Eyes"   Mr. Big
8. "Home Sweet Home"   Pretty Boy Floyd
9. "Honestly"   Shark Island
10. "House of Pain"   Sleeze Beez
11. "I Wanna Be With You"   Stryper
12. "Out of Love"   Warrant
13. "This Time"   White Lion
14. "To Be With You"   Whitesnake
15. "The Ballad of Jayne"   Winger

HEAVY METAL CHICKS

Let's face it, one of the best things about metal back in the '80s was the girls. And we're not talking about the typical rode hard and put away wet groupies who will always be found at rock concerts. We're talking about all the hot chicks with the skin tight leather pants, enormous hairdos, and makeup. Wait a minute, that was the guys. Nevertheless, there were tons of beautiful girls in the videos and at the concerts drooling over all of the pretty boy singers like Bon Jovi, Jani Lane, and Udo. Now granted, the women were probably slightly more attractive at say a White Lion concert than a Motorhead show, but I'm sure Lemmy had his fare share of babes, too. Well, this section is dedicated to all of those fine women, featuring songs related to those irreplaceable heavy metal chicks!

1. "Can I Sit Next To You Girl"	AC/DC
2. "Carrie"	Alice Cooper
3. "Charlotte the Harlot"	Cats in Boots
4. "Christine Sixteen"	Europe
5. "Heavy Metal Love"	Helix
6. "Little Suzi"	Iron Maiden
7. "Madelaine"	KISS
8. "Magdalaine"	L.A. Guns
9. "Only Women Bleed"	Tesla
10. "Shotgun Sally"	Winger

WELCOME TO THE JUNGLE

Guns N' Roses is one of the greatest rock bands to ever strap on guitars and invade the Sunset Strip. Pioneering sleaze metal with the likes of L.A. Guns and Faster Pussycat, they brought a stripped-down debaucherous attitude that rivaled Mötley Crüe, but without the hairspray. Except maybe for Axl in "Welcome to the Jungle," but we'll give him a pass since it also introduced the world to the famous Axl Shuffle.

Sprouting from the remnants of Hollywood Rose & L.A. Guns, they exploded out of the box, sending their debut album straight to #1 thanks to three Top Ten hits. When they first hit the scene, it was a breath of fresh air. While stopping at a record store to check out some new releases, we heard some great new music playing. When we asked who the band was, we were informed it was a new band out of Los Angeles, Guns N' Roses. This was followed up with the bold prediction, "These guys are gonna be bigger than Poison!"

We became instant fans along with the rest of the world. The exception being the group of students riding the Daytona Spring Break party bus with us. After someone played CCR's greatest hits on his boom box for the hundredth time, we decided to introduce everyone to GNR's debut masterpiece. They weren't happy. Granted, it was about 3:00 in the morning and everyone was mostly drunk, hung-over and asleep, but still.

As with any good rock band, controversy seemed to follow them. In fact, they took it to a whole new level. It started with their very first album cover. Many distributors were upset by the sexually violent artwork, so it had to be moved to the inside and replaced with the classic cross and skulls cover. Their second record was even more controversial. Despite featuring the massive hit "Patience," it also included "Used to Love Her" which many people viewed as misogynistic thanks to the "but I had to kill her" lyric. Even worse, the album featured the song "One in a Million" which was hailed as being both racist and homophobic, complete with the now taboo "N-word". Even a simple album of cover tunes couldn't avoid trouble thanks to the inclusion of a hidden track written by, of all people, Charles Manson.

The controversies weren't limited to their music and artwork. Most of the band members struggled with substance abuse and there were plenty of arrests, including Axl's for biting a security guard on the leg! Then there was the 1992 St. Louis riot. Angered that security wasn't stopping someone from taking pictures, Axl leaped off the stage, tackled the photographer, took his camera, hit several people with it then took off, refusing to finish the show. Fans were not amused and a three-hour riot ensued. Later that year they caused another riot in Montreal when they played a show with Metallica, who had to cut their set short when James Hetfield suffered serious burns from their pyro. Axl showed up late and then walked off the stage after only an hour complaining about vocal issues. The result was another riot to the tune of nearly half a million dollars in damages.

That same year, we were fortunate enough to see them with Soundgarden opening. Sure enough, that show nearly turned into a riot, as well. Axl was habitually late, and we knew we were in trouble when the tickets didn't specify a start time, but simply stated the show would start "around" 8:00. Well, Soundgarden didn't even hit the stage until 9:00. They played for an hour and then the wait was on. Not thirty minutes like most shows. Not an hour or even an hour and a half. No, Axl and the boys didn't hit the stage for two full hours, finally starting at midnight! Not surprisingly, fans started getting very restless in those two long hours and began voicing their disappointment. Things got so bad Slash came out on stage to apologize, blaming technical problems. Fortunately, the venue decided not to sell any alcohol. Good thing. A bunch of drunk rockers would've torn that place apart. To their credit, when they finally hit the stage, they played for a good two and a half hours, ending at 2:30 in the morning. Needless to say, we didn't make our 8:00 a.m. class in the morning. We were all broken up about it, as you can imagine.

Of course, Guns N' Roses wouldn't have become the legends they are if not for their incredible music and the ability to soldier on despite a revolving door of musicians. Guitarists alone have included a Slash, Izzy, Bumblefoot and Buckethead among others. And despite all of the instability, the numbers don't lie. *Appetite for Destruction* has sold over 30 million copies with "Sweet Child O' Mine" going to #1 on the *Billboard Hot 100*. Their follow-up, *G N' R Lies* sold 10 million and the two *Use Your Illusion* albums debuted at #1 and #2 on the Billboard 200, selling over 35 million units combined. Even their last album, the divisive *Chinese Democracy* debuted at #3 on the Billboard 200.

And 35 years after the release of their first record, they're still going strong. They were inducted into the Rock and Roll Hall of Fame in 2012. Slash reunited with Axl in 2016, after 23 years apart. That same year Axl ended up fronting AC/DC briefly when their singer suffered serious hearing issues. In 2021 they released two new songs and in 2022 they are still touring the world, bringing the jungle everywhere they go.

CHAPTER 11
CRANK IT TO 11 - METAL IN THE MOVIES

Lucky for us fans of hard rock, not all movies choose to feature such head banging tunes as "Chariots of Fire." In fact, some soundtracks contain nothing but hard rock. You might even remember a certain horror writer who featured one single hard rock band for the soundtrack to his entire movie. We believe he made the comment that the world's scariest movie needed the world's loudest band. Well, the movie part of the comment wasn't exactly true, but he got pretty close about the band. We'd elaborate further, but it would give away the answer to one of the questions below. So grab some popcorn, your favorite beverage, or maybe something to mix with your favorite beverage, conspicuously concealed in your coat pocket, and get ready to sneak into the back door of your local movie theater because the lights are starting to dim and the feature presentation is about to begin.

1. *Light of Day* was a 1987 movie starring Michael J. Fox and what female rocker?
A. Lita Ford
B. Joan Jett
C. Janet Gardner
D. Boy George

2. "Cemetary Gates" from *Tales From the Crypt Presents: Demon Knight* is a song by what band?
A. Slayer
B. Pantera
C. Exodus
D. The Rock Bottom Remainders

3. "Flash of the Blade" from Dario Argenta's horror film *Phenomenon* is a song by which metal band?
A. Judas Priest
B. Dark August
C. Iron Maiden
D. Flash Gordon

4. "Love is a Lie" was the recording debut by what metal band for the soundtrack to *Friday the 13th Part 4*?
A. Dokken
B. Lion
C. King's X
D. Flaming Lips

5. Alice Cooper had a minor comeback with the song "Man Behind the Mask" from what classic horror movie series?
A. *Halloween 3*
B. *Friday the 13th (Part VI)*
C. *Nightmare on Elm Street 2*
D. *The Brady Bunch*

6. Alice Cooper's classic "No More Mr. Nice Guy" was redone by a speed metal band for inclusion onto what electrifying horror movie soundtrack?

A. *Halloween*

B. *Friday the 13th*

C. *Shocker*

D. *The Sound of Music*

7. Bang Tango's song "I'm a Stranger" appeared on the soundtrack to what 1988 movie about demons posing as a rock band?

A. *Black Roses*

B. *Stone Roses*

C. *Black Stallion*

D. *Black Bean Soup*

8. Before actually calling themselves Velvet Revolver they recorded the song "Set Me Free" for inclusion on what movie soundtrack?

A. *The Hulk*

B. *Last Action Hero*

C. *Airheads*

D. *Ishtar*

9. Cinderella, Bulletboys, Black Sabbath, Alice Cooper and Rhino Bucket all provide songs to what party (on) movie?

A. *Wayne's World*

B. *Airheads*

C. *Wayne's World 2*

D. *Toy Story*

10. For what movie did Jon Bon Jovi sing "Blaze of Glory"?
A. *Young Guns*
B. *Young Guns II*
C. *Billy the Kid*
D. *The Karate Kid*

11. For which movie did Guns N' Roses record a cover of the Rolling Stones tune "Symphony for the Devil"?
A. *The Vampire Lestat*
B. *Interview with the Vampire*
C. *Bram Stroker's Dracula*
D. *Little Dracula*

12. In the 1986 movie *Crossroads*, what famous musician was pitted against Ralph Machio in the guitar duel for his soul?
A. Joe Satriani
B. Steve Vai
C. Yngwie J. Malmsteen
D. Homer Simpson

13. In what 1985 comedy did Twisted Sister appear while singing the song "Burn in Hell"?
A. *Pee Wee's Big Adventure*
B. *Back To The Future*
C. *The Goonies*
D. *The Color Purple*

14. In what Arnold Schwarzenegger movie did the lead singer of Little Caesar portray a tattooed, tough biker who got into a fight with The Governator?
A. *Commando*
B. *Last Action Hero*
C. *Terminator 2*
D. *Fast Action Zero*

15. Marc Storace co-starred with Doro Pesch in what Swiss movie about a hunter from the Bronze Age?

A. *Transformers*

B. *Power Rangers*

C. *Anuk-The Path of the Warrior*

D. *Debbie Does Dishes*

16. Motorhead, Ice T and Ugly Kid Joe's Whitfield Crane re-recorded "Born to Raise Hell" for which popular Adam Sandler movie?

A. *Airheads*

B. *Billy Madison*

C. *The Wedding Singer*

D. *The Price is Right*

17. Name Rob Reiner's famous pseudo "Rockumentary" about an aging rock band.

A. *This Is Spinal Tap*

B. *Hello, Cleveland*

C. *Metal: A Headbanger's Journey*

D. *This is Beer Tap*

18. Name the "band" consisting of legendary rockers Paul Stanley, Rudy Sarzo, Vivian Campbell and Tommy Lee, who sang the title track to the Wes Craven horror film, *Shocker*.

A. Dudes of Wrath

B. Wrathchild

C. All the Young Dudes

D. Grapes of Wrath

19. Name the 1984 Michael Crichton thriller, which starred Tom Selleck and founding KISS member Gene Simmons as Dr. Charles Luther, about killer robots.
A. *Trick or Treat*
B. *Runaway*
C. *Sphere*
D. *Quigley Down Under*

20. Sammy Hagar had a popular song from what Sylvester Stallone arm wrestling movie?
A. *Cobra*
B. *The Champ*
C. *Over the Top*
D. *Rambo Balboa*

21. Saraya's "Timeless Love" was featured in what Wes Craven movie?
A. *Scream*
B. *Shocker*
C. *A Nightmare on Elm Street*
D. *A Shocker on Scream Street*

22. Shark Island had two songs, "Dangerous" and "Father Time", that appeared on what comedy film's soundtrack?
A. *Bill and Ted's Excellent Adventure*
B. *Bill and Ted's Bogus Journey*
C. *Back To The Future*
D. *Platoon*

23. *Some Kind of Monster* is the critically acclaimed 2004 documentary of what band?
A. Metallica
B. Cheap Trick
C. Monster Magnet
D. Herman's Munsters

24. Spinal Tap's lead singer was better known as what character in the '70s thanks to a *Happy Days* spin-off?
A. Lenny from *Laverne & Shirley*
B. Squiggy from *Laverne & Shirley*
C. Mearth from *Mork & Mindy*
D. Al from *Joanie Loves Chachi*

25. The demo version of the Pretty Boy Floyd tune "48 Hours" appeared on the soundtrack to what 1989 film?
A. *The Karate Kid, Part II*
B. *The Karate Kid*
C. *The Karate Kid, Part III*
D. *The Karate Squid*

26. The heavy metal band Keel sang "Rock 'N' Roll Outlaw" for what 1987 Penelope Spheeris movie starring John Cryer?
A. *Young Guns*
B. *Christine*
C. *Dudes*
D. *Pretty in Pink*

27. The Joe Satriani song "One Big Rush" was featured on the soundtrack to what Cameron Crowe hit movie from 1989?
A. *Sixteen Candles*
B. *Say Anything*
C. *Better Off Dead*
D. *Breakfast at Tiffany's*

28. The KISS disco classic "I Was Made For Lovin' You" was featured on the soundtrack to what classic early '80s movie starring Brooke Shields?
A. *The Blue Lagoon*
B. *Endless Love*
C. *Tilt*
D. *Pretty Baby Bop*

29. The Montrose hit "Rock Candy" can be heard in which 1976 Barbra Streisand film as she arrives backstage?
A. *A Star is Born*
B. *Funny Girl*
C. *The Way We Were*
D. *A Porn Star is Born*

30. The Motorhead song "You Better Run" was re-recorded in 2004 as "You Better Swim" for what movie?
A. *Finding Nemo*
B. *Shark Tales*
C. *The SpongeBob SquarePants Movie*
D. *Jaws*

31. The new, unpublicized Guns 'N Roses song "Oh My God" appeared on the soundtrack to what movie?
A. *The Ring*
B. *School of Rock*
C. *End of Days*
D. *Gone With the Wind*

32. The Planet Us song "Vertigo" was written for what super hero movie?
A. *Batman Returns*
B. *The X-Men*
C. *Spider-Man*
D. *Mermaid Man & Barnacle Boy*

33. The Ratt song "Nobody Rides for Free" was featured in what classic 1991 Patrick Swayze/Keanu Reeves flick along with songs by Shark Island, Westworld, L.A. Guns, Little Caesar and others?
A. *Point Break*
B. *Red Dawn*
C. *Ghost*
D. *Red Bull*

34. The singer for what metal band actually provided the vocals for the main character in *Rock Star*?

A. Every Mother's Nightmare
B. Steelheart
C. Lillian Axe
D. The Beach Boys

35. The three main actors in Spinal Tap appeared in yet another mockumentary called *A Mighty Wind* in 2003 as an American folk revival band. What was their band's name?

A. Peter, Paul, & Harry
B. The Folksmen
C. Bedlelly
D. Metallica

36. W.A.S.P.'s "Scream Until You Like It" was the theme song to what gremlinesque movie?

A. *C.H.U.D.*
B. *Gremlins II*
C. *Goulies II*
D. *Casablanca*

37. What 1981 animated movie soundtrack consisted entirely of rock tunes by such artists as Black Sabbath, Cheap Trick and Blue Oyster Cult?

A. *Heavy Metal*
B. *Metal Mania*
C. *The Decline of Western Civilization*
D. *Spongebob Squaepants*

38. What all-female rock band had songs featured in the movies *Detroit Rock City, Dawn: Portrait of a Teenage Runaway*, and *Dazed and Confused?*
A. The Cherry Bombs
B. Warlock
C. The Runaways
D. The Spice Girls

39. What award-winning actor starred as Bret Michael's father in the 1998 movie that he wrote and starred in?
A. Marlon Brando
B. Donald Sutherland
C. Martin Sheen
D. George Jetson

40. What was the name of the movie that was inspired by the real life story of Judas Priest hiring a Priest cover band singer as their singer?
A. *Rock Star*
B. *Almost Famous*
C. *Slaves to the Underground*
D. *King Kong*

41. What band recorded the theme song for the animated 1986 film, *The Transformers: The Movie?*
A. Lion
B. Van Halen
C. Arcade
D. The Clash

42. What band sang the song "Love Kills" for *A Nightmare On Elm Street 4: The Dream Master?*
A. Dokken
B. Metallica
C. Vinnie Vincent Invasion
D. Freddy & The Fishsticks

43. What Black Sabbath tune featuring Ronnie James Dio appeared on their *Dehumanizer* album as well as the *Wayne's World* soundtrack?
A. "The Wizard"
B. "Mob Rules"
C. "Time Machine"
D. "Iron Woman"

44. What excellent 1991 film featured the KISS song "God Gave Rock N' Roll to You II" and "The Reaper" by Steve Vai?
A. *Bill & Ted's Bogus Journey*
B. *Bill & Ted's Excellent Adventure*
C. *Bill & Ted Face the Music*
D. *Bill & Ted's Gnarly Roadtrip*

45. What guitarist won the Adult Video Network award for best movie soundtrack in 2006?
A. Eddie Van Halen
B. Steve Vai
C. Joe Satriani
D. Chuck Berry

46. What is the name of the 1980 movie about rock groupie Lola Bouilliabase trying to make it with the legendary Alice Cooper (who appears as himself in the movie) which also stars Meat Loaf as Travis W. Redfish?
A. *Roadie*
B. *Rock & Roll High School*
C. *Almost Famous*
D. *Beach Blanket Bingo*

47. What is the name of the filmmaker responsible for the *Decline of Western Civilization* series of films?
A. Terry Micheals
B. Penelope Spheeris
C. Penelope Cruz
D. Alf

48. What is the name of the 1994 moving starring Adam Sandler, Brendan Fraser, and Steve Buscemi as a rock trio that holds a radio station hostage so that they'll play their song on the air?
A. *Rock Star*
B. *Airheads*
C. *Rock and Roll High School*
D. *Saved By the Bell*

49. What is the name of the 2008 movie featuring Queensrÿche's Geoff Tate and Blackmore's Night singer Candice Night?
A. *The Hills Have Eyes*
B. *House of Eternity*
C. *Nightmare*
D. *Gone With the Window*

50. What is the name of the hot band featured in *The Decline of Western Civilization Part 2* that never lived up to the movie's expectations?
A. Odin
B. Omen
C. Gargantuan
D. Seals & Crofts

51. What is the name of the tribute band in the movie *Rock Star*?
A. Steel Dragon
B. Monster
C. Blood Pollution
D. Kentucky Headhunters

52. What John Cusack movie featured a guitar weilding hamburger jamming to Van Halen's "And the Cradle Will Rock"?
A. *Cradle Will Rock*
B. *Say Anything*
C. *Better Off Dead*
D. *Women and Hamburgers First*

53. What metal band performed the song "Dream Warriors" for the 3rd *Nightmare on Elm Street* movie?
A. Dokken
B. Ratt
C. Dream Theater
D. Freddy & The Fishsticks

54. What metal band provided the soundtrack to the horror flick *Trick or Treat*?
A. KISS
B. Frehley's Comet
C. Fastway
D. Wham!

55. What metal band sang "It's Too Late" from the soundtrack to *Iron Eagle*?
A. Dokken
B. Helix
C. L.A. Guns
D. Menudo

56. What metal singer acted in the movies *Never Too Young To Die* and *Bad Channels*?
A. Jon Bon Jovi
B. Ron Keel
C. Ronnie James Dio
D. Clay Aiken

57. What movie marked the acting debut of Ronnie James Dio?
A. *Tenacious D in The Pick of Destiny*
B. *School of Rock*
C. *Airheads*
D. *Gone With The Windows*

58. What movie soundtrack featured the Pantera/Rob Halford collaboration "Light Comes Out of Black?"
A. *Halloween H2O*
B. *Shocker*
C. *Buffy the Vampire Slayer*
D. *The Sound of Music*

59. What musical style was showcased in the classic music documentary *The Decline of Western Civilization Part II?*
A. Punk Rock
B. Heavy Metal
C. Hard Rock
D. Swing

60. What song appears on both the *Rock Star* soundtrack as well as Steelheart's 3rd album *Wait?*
A. "Never Let You Go"
B. "Eileen"
C. "We all Die Young"
D. "Knick Knack Paddy Wack"

61. What Tom Hanks movie did White Lion perform in with a female singer before they recorded their debut album?
A. *The Money Pit*
B. *Bachelor Party*
C. *Splash*
D. *Saving Ryan's Privates*

62. What was the movie *Rock Star* originally going to be called?
A. *Rocker*
B. *Metal God*
C. *We Rock*
D. *No Brown M&M's*

63. What was the name of Led Zeppelin's famous 1976 concert film?

A. *Coda*

B. *Physcial Graffiti*

C. *The Song Remains The Same*

D. *Grease*

64. What was the name of the 1986 documentary about fans tailgating before a Judas Priest/Dokken concert in Landover, Maryland?

A. *Living After Midnight*

B. *Chasing Tailgate*

C. *Heavy Metal Parking Lot*

D. *Roger Rabbit and Me*

65. What was the name of the 1987 dark comedy by the makers of the TV show *The Young Ones* which included a performance by Motorhead and featured Lemmy in a role as a character named Spider?

A. *Eat the Rich*

B. *Edge of Seventeen*

C. *Pacific Heights*

D. *The Wizard of Oz*

66. What was the name of the 1990 movie tracking the success of four members of the KISS Army trying to attend a 1978 KISS concert without tickets?

A. *Cold Gin Time*

B. *Detroit Rock City*

C. *Strutter*

D. *Mandy*

67. What was the name of the 1998 psychological thriller that Bret Michaels wrote and starred in?

A. *Strangeland*

B. *A Letter From Death Row*

C. *Letter to the Editor*

D. *C is for Cookie*

68. What was the name of the commercially successful 1978 made-for-TV movie starring KISS as themselves who had secret talisman amulets that gave them special powers capable of defeating evil android look-alikes? No, seriously...

A. *KISS Meets the Phantom of the Park*

B. *The Elder*

C. *KISS Meets the Phantom of the Dark*

D. *KISS Meets Scooby Doo*

69. What was the name of the famous 1988 biography about heavy metal which was a follow-up to the filmmaker's 1981 documentary about punk rock?

A. *The Decline of Western Civilization*

B. *The Decline of Western Civilization Part II: The Metal Years*

C. *The Decline of Western Civilization Part III: The Metal Monsters*

D. *The Decline of Western & Southern*

70. What was the name of the fictional band in the movie *Rock Star*?

A. Dragonforce

B. Red Dragons

C. Steel Dragon

D. Dragon Breath

71. What was the name of the main character in the movie *Rock Star*?
A. Ozzy
B. Dizzy
C. Izzy
D. Fuzzy Wuzzy

72. What band had their previously unreleased song "Slam Dunk" appear on the soundtrack to the 1991 Ellen Barkin movie *Switch*?
A. DLR Band
B. Kix
C. Pretty Boy Floyd
D. The Harlem Globetrotters

73. Which member of KISS made a brief appearance as a radio disc jockey in the horror film *Trick or Treat*?
A. Gene Simmons
B. Paul Stanley
C. Ace Frehley
D. Wolfman Jack

74. Which Stephen King movie starring Emilio Estevez, used all AC/DC songs for its entire soundtrack?
A. *Salem's Lot*
B. *Maximum Overdrive*
C. *Pet Semetary*
D. *The Mighty Ducks*

75. While giving dating advice in the classic movie *Fast Times at Ridgemont High*, Damone told Mark to play side one of what classic Led Zeppelin album?
A. *Led Zeppelin III*
B. *Led Zeppelin II*
C. *Led Zeppelin IV*
D. *Dread Zeppelin II*

THE RISING SWEDISH GUITAR FORCE

For our next two stories, we'll discuss two legendary artists who have had intertwining careers. Two artists we've seen live, one we've met and the other, well, you'll have to keep reading. This story is about Swedish guitar virtuoso, Yngwie J. Malmsteen. What does the "J." stand for? Good question. You'll find it in Chapter Two. The next story is about the incredible vocalist, Joe Lynn Turner. Turner sang on Yngwie's 1988 solo album *Odyssey* which is his highest charting release on the Billboard charts. It boasted the popular single "Heaven Tonight." Joe also sang on Yngwie's 1989 live album as well as his 1996 album *Inspiration.*

Yngwie first played with a band called Steeler in the early '80s. He then joined Alcatrazz and played on their first album. Unfortunately, he fought with the band's singer. That wouldn't be the last time he clashed with a vocalist.

Yngwie really found fame when he released his first solo album *Rising Force* in 1984, later receiving a Grammy for his work. From that point on, his neo-classical shredding became legendary, and his name is often mentioned along with other metal guitar masters like Steve Vai, Joe Satriani, and Randy Rhodes.

Over the past four decades, he released a whopping twenty-one studio albums. He also developed a reputation of being a bit arrogant, as well as difficult to work with. Perhaps that's why he now plays most of the instruments himself on his albums. He not only plays guitar, but he also plays bass, drums, keyboards, organ, cello, and sitar. He also provides all vocals on his albums. Like him or not, you can't deny he's a talented guy!

In 2022, we finally had a chance to see Yngwie perform at the famous M3 Rock Festival. We had VIP tickets and were excited about the prospect of possibly meeting him. We wanted to learn firsthand who he really was! We were lucky enough to meet a lot of great performers that day including Doro, Stephen Pearcy, Tony Harnell from TNT, Lillian Axe, Leatherwolf, Zebra, and more.

As soon as they announced his meet-and-greet, fans lined up quickly and in large numbers. Fortunately, we were near the front. So, we all waited. And we waited. And we waited some more. Finally, we saw some activity and the crowd started buzzing with excitement. After waiting close to an hour and missing most of XYZ's set, a gentleman finally emerged from the meet-and-greet area and announced, "Yngwie will not be participating in today's meet-and-greet." No reason given. Classic.

Despite not meeting him, we still showed up later to watch him perform. It was quite loud, and his guitar was up very high in the mix, but his band was excellent. His guitar playing was impeccable, and he threw out lots of picks. Kicked out would be more accurate, although many of the picks never made it past the security barrier. He displayed his vocal talent by singing "Smoke on the Water." He's a better guitar player than a singer, but he actually sounded pretty decent. The set was enjoyable. Hopefully, one day we'll get a chance to finally meet him, with or without his signature Stratocaster.

CHAPTER 12
EXIT STAGE NAMES LEFT

We had so much fun writing the last matching chapter that we just had to write another one. And we're sure you had fun drawing all of those connecting lines. You know, if you draw all of the lines correctly, and you put on the *Dark Side of the Moon* at the beginning of the *Wizard of Oz* then you will actually draw a picture of the Mona Lisa or maybe it just looks that way if you've had too many of those beverages we talked about in the last matching chapter. By the way, we sure hope you used a pencil to draw your matching lines instead of a Sharpie, so that someone else could borrow your book and draw their own lines. On second thought, we'd rather them buy their own book. Let us suggest a black Sharpie, extra fine point.

NICKNAMES

This is a matching section about nicknames. Questions about Nick Carter from NSYNC and questions about Nickleback and what is Saint Nicholas' real name. Okay, so that's not what this section is really about. Actually, it's quite simple. You just have to match a musician to their nickname. But not to be confused with the next section where you will be matching an artist to their stage name. You see, a nickname is different than their stage name. A nickname is just an alternative name they some-times go by where a stage name is the actual name that they use to identify themselves even if it isn't their real name. Do you know who The King of All Badasses is? You'll get your chance to guess below.

1. Diamond Dave	Michael Henry McBrain
2. Bonzo	Rob Hunter
3. Wacko	David Lee Roth
4. Dimebag	Dave Evans
5. Fast	Darrell Abbott
6. Fingers	Eddie Ojeda
7. King	Eddie Clarke
8. Nicko	
9. Philthy Animal	John Bonham
10. Sex	Phil Taylor
11. Steamin'	Steve Clark
12. The Animal	Steve Summers
13. The King of All	Mark Mendoza
Badasses	Robbin Crosby
14. Ripper	Jeff Warner
15. Woop	Tim Owens

STAGE NAMES

As we've already established, image sells. Entertainers from musicians to actors have modified their real names to create a more glamorous image. Norma Jean became Marilyn Monroe and J.P. Richardson became the Big Bopper. Big hair artists were no exception. Many of the popular artists used stage names.

Let's face it; their mothers didn't put "Buckethead" or "Slash" on their kids' birth certificates. Shocking, we know. We apologize for breaking this earth shattering news to you. But hey, it's not like we spoiled the ending to the last Harry Potter book where Harry has a sex change operation and becomes Harriet Potter. Oops. But seriously folks, we know that this section is hard. Really hard. Harder than finding a white t-shirt at a Metallica concert hard. We don't expect you to know all of these answers, of course. Maybe not even half of them. But we think you'll find them interesting. You might just learn something. You can even tell your friends that you're not just reading a trivia book, you're conducting academic research. They'll be so impressed. So take your seats, the bell is ringing and class is about to begin.

Our memorable
Meet-and-Greet with
Joe Lynn Turner

1. Alice Cooper	Bret Sychak
2. Axl Rose	Brian Carroll
3. Bobby Dall	Bruce Anthony Johannesson
4. Buckethead	Chaim Witz
5. Bumblefoot	Colin Flooks
6. C.C. Deville	Frank Feranna, Jr.
7. Cozy Powell	Jakey Lou Williams
8. Eric Carr	James Southworth
9. Gene Simmons	Jeffrey Dean Isbell
10. Izzy Stradlin	Jim Wilkinson
11. Jake E. Lee	Joseph Bellardini
12. Jizzy Pearl	Joseph Linquito
13. Joe Lynn Turner	Mark Norton
14. Joey Belladonna	Nicholas Dingley
15. Mark St. John	Paul Caravello
16. Mick Mars	Richard Allan Ream
17. Nikki Sixx	Robert Deal
18. Paul Stanley	Robert Harry Kuykendall
19. Rachel Bolan	Ron Thal
20. Razzle	Ronald Padavona
21. Rikki Rockett	Sandi Salvador
22. Ronnie James Dio	Saul Hudson
23. Saraya	Stanley Eisen
24. Slash	Thomas Bass
25. Bret Michaels	Timothy Hagelganz
26. Timothy Gaines	Tracy Ulrich
27. Tommy Lee	Vincent Cusano
28. Tracii Guns	Vincent Furnier
29. Vince Neil	Vincent Wharton
30. Vinnie Vincent	William Bailey

STREET OF DREAMS

Joe Lynn Turner was a beloved rock and roll singer for decades. He first achieved fame when he joined the legendary Rainbow in 1980. With big shoes to fill, Turner replaced Graham Bonnet who sang on Rainbow's first big hit "Since You've Been Gone." Bonnet had replaced Ronnie James Dio.

Turner provided vocals for three of Rainbow's most commercially successful albums. They featured such hits as "I Surrender," "Stone Cold," and "Street of Dreams." As mentioned previously, Joe also sang on Yngwie's most successful album. Ironically, the first time we saw Turner live was at the first Melodicrock Festival where he sang a duet of "Since You've Been Gone" with another former Yngwie vocalist, Jeff Scott Soto. What a collaboration!

After singing for Rainbow and Yngwie, JLT, often referred to by his initials, has been extremely prolific. He sang on Deep Purple's 1990 *Masters and Slaves* album. He also sung on albums for Mother's Army, Brazen Abbot, Sunstorm, as well as a dozen solo albums. He sung lead or backing vocals for an unbelievable number of artists covering a wide range of styles. Everything from the metal bands like Bonfire, Riot and TNT, to the not-so-metal artists like Cher, Michael Bolton, and Billy Joel.

We were fortunate enough to see him perform at a small club in Cincinnati in 2017. It was a little college bar that often booked local, blues, rock, and EDM bands. How he ended up there is anybody's guess. The show was so poorly promoted there appeared to be more fans there to support the local opening band than for JLT. It was a bit depressing, but when he hit the stage, it might as well have been Madison Square Garden. He played to the small crowd like he was performing in front of 50,000 people. He sounded amazing, and the set list was a rocker's dream. He sang mostly Rainbow songs, a couple of Deep Purple songs, and even two Yngwie songs. Surprisingly, "Heaven Tonight" was not one of them. He appeared to be having just as much fun as the fans!

After the show, the promoter announced meet-and-greet with Mr. Turner for a mere $50. Not having a spare fifty bucks, we, along with our friend Russell, went outside and chatted awhile. We were standing right next to the meet-and-greet line. So instead of standing *near* it, we decided to stand *in* it. The promoter noticed and asked the three of us if we'd like to meet Joe Lynn Turner. Sure! But we didn't have the necessary $150. We had already spent our cash inside.

The promoter pulled us aside and quietly asked us how much money we *did* have. Turns out, not much. Don was the tycoon with thirteen dollars! Russ had 50 cents and Ron had nothing. He said, "Fine, give me everything you've got." He even took the two quarters. For less than five bucks apiece, we met the iconic vocalist, got his autograph, and a group picture. And as we had expected, he was kind and engaging. Ron interviewed him years ago, and he was just as friendly.

When we asked how it felt to play to such a small crowd, he said it was no big deal because he was heading back to Europe soon where he'd be playing in front of tens of thousands. Of the hundreds of concerts we've seen over the years, this was one of the best. And thanks to the set list we peeled off the stage, we'll always remember every song he played!

CHAPTER 13
WHO THE F*&# ARE YOU?

For this next section, we get to cover the heaviest band on the planet, The Who! Okay, not exactly. This section is really all about owls! No? Would you believe, the Indianapolis Hoosiers? Okay, okay, seriously–these questions are all about "Who did this?" and "Who did that?" in the world of hard rocking metal. You know, "Who did Pamela Anderson?" and "Who drank too much?" Well, actually, those questions would have too many answers so we'll stick to other "who" related questions. So grab some Green Eggs and Spam because we're off to WHOville!

1. In 2006, who became the new lead singer of TNT after the departure of the band's long-time singer?
A. Tony Harnell
B. Tony Hansen
C. Tony Mills
D. Tony the Tiger

2. Once a singer for Journey, who was the original vocalist for the Vinnie Vincent Invasion?
A. Steve Perry
B. Robert Fleischman
C. Steve Augeri
D. Steve Augeri Perry

3. Who is the metal vocalist who is also a trained pilot for air flight company Astraeus?
A. Geoff Tate
B. Rob Halford
C. Bruce Dickinson
D. John Travolta

4. Who appears as the guest vocalist on the song "The Chase" from Queensrÿche's 2006 album *Operation: Mindcrime II*?
A. Jeff Scott Soto
B. Ronnie James Dio
C. Joe Lynn Turner
D. Tina Turner

5. Who are the German rockers that sang the song "All We Are"?
A. Warlock
B. Scorpions
C. Bonfire
D. All We Are The World

6. Who claimed "Rock and Roll (Is Gonna Set the Night on Fire)"?
A. Pretty Boy Floyd
B. Slaughter
C. KISS
D. Smoky the Bear

7. Who claimed that "Love Ain't Easy"?
A. Tesla
B. White Lion
C. Steelheart
D. Larry King

8. Who did Phil Lewis replace as lead singer of the L.A. Guns?
A. Paul White
B. Paul Black
C. Jeff White
D. Jack Black

9. Who had "All The Time in the World"?
A. Alias
B. Junkyard
C. Bullet Boys
D. Morris Day

10. Who had a "Green-Tinted Sixties Mind"?
A. Blind Melon
B. Mr. Big
C. Extreme
D. Wavy Gravy

11. Who has a baby seal as their mascot?
A. Raven
B. Krokus
C. RIOT
D. Heidi Klum

12. Who hated "Everything About You"?
A. Ugly Kid Joe
B. Green Jelly
C. The Flaming Lips
D. Ugly Kid Rock

13. Who is "The Voice of Rock"?
A. Billy Squier
B. Glenn Hughes
C. Joe Lynn Turner
D. Kaptain Kangaroo

14. Who is "Herman Ze German"?
A. Herman Meine
B. Herman Schenker
C. Herman Rarebell
D. Herman Munster

15. Who is listed as the guitarist on Pantera's *Cowboys From Hell* album?
A. Dimebag Darrell
B. Diamond Darrell
C. Darrell Abbott
D. Darrell, Darrell & My Other Brother Darrell

16. Who is Pamela Moore better known as to metal-heads?
A. Sister Mary
B. Joan Jett
C. Gary Moore's wife
D. Ginger Grant

17. Who is the wife of Gene Simmons?
A. Shannon Stewart
B. Shannon Tweed
C. Heather Locklear
D. Shannen Doherty

18. Who is the artist that trained to be a foil fencer before becoming a singer, has a father that is one of the world's best known children's book illustrators and once appeared on the children's television show *Wonderama?*
A. Bruce Dickinson
B. Dee Snider
C. Danny Vaughn
D. Zorro Pesch

19. Who is the guest vocalist on Def Leppard's rendition of the Sweet tune "Hell Raiser" on their all covers album?
A. Brian Connolly
B. Justin Hawkins
C. Axl Rose
D. Florence Jean Castleberry

20. Who is the metal-head with a younger sister named Athena Kottak who is also the drummer for a band named KrunK?
A. Tommy Lee
B. Jeff Keith
C. Bruce Dickinson
D. Barney Fife

21. Who is the self-proclaimed "Metal God"?
A. Rob Halford
B. Ronnie James Dio
C. Ozzy Osbourne
D. Michael Bublé

22. Who is the singer of Van Helsing's Curse?
A. Sammy Hagar
B. Bruce Dickinson
C. Dee Snider
D. Dracula

23. Who played guitar on Ozzy's 2005 album *Under Cover?*
A. Jerry Cantrell
B. Zakk Wylde
C. Jake E. Lee
D. Jerry Springer

24. Who is the vocalist that has sung for ARK, Masterplan, Millennium, The Snakes and Vagabond?
A. Russell Allen
B. Michael Kiske
C. Jorn Lande
D. John Tesh

25. Who played plumber Victor Morrison, a love interest to TV's Ally McBeal?
A. Sebastian Bach
B. Jason Bonham
C. Jon Bon Jovi
D. Snyder

26. Who played the drums for the Led Zeppelin reunion show on Nov. 26, 2007?
A. Phil Collins
B. Ringo Starr
C. Jason Bonham
D. Betty Rubble

27. Who produced the Sea Hags' demo tape?
A. Kirk Hammett
B. Gene Simmons
C. Clive Davis
D. Popeye

28. Who produced Van Halen's original demo?
A. Eddie Van Halen
B. Gene Simmons
C. Clive Davis
D. Ann B. Davis

29. Who provides the voice for "The Kid" in Babylon A.D.'s song "The Kid Goes Wild"?
A. Steve Martin
B. Bill Murray
C. Sam Kinison
D. Mr. Bill

30. Who received the KOSA Lifetime Achievement Award for rock drumming in 2007?
A. Neil Peart
B. Carmine Appice
C. Alex Van Halen
D. Animal

31. Who replaced Ace Frehley when he was ousted from KISS (the first time)?
A. Mark St. John
B. Bruce Kulick
C. Vinnie Vincent
D. Chris Gaines

32. Who replaced Adrian Smith as guitarist in Iron Maiden, appearing on their 1990 album *No Prayer for the Dying*?
A. Janick Gers
B. Dave Murray
C. Nicko McBrain
D. Yo, Adrian!

33. Who replaced Bruce Dickinson as lead vocalist for Iron Maiden?
A. Paul Di'Anno
B. Paul Laine
C. Blaze Bayley
D. Paul Bunyan

34. Who replaced fired Dream Theater keyboardist Derek Sherinian in 1999?
A. Jordan Rudess
B. Gregg Giuffria
C. Jordan Sas
D. Michael Jordan

35. Who replaced Joe Perry when he left Aerosmith in 1979?
A. Jimmy Vaughn
B. Jimmy Crespo
C. Jimmy Clarke
D. Jimmy Carter

36. Who replaced Night Ranger's long-standing guitarist Jeff Watson in 2007?
A. John Norum
B. Reb Beach
C. Jake E. Lee
D. Minnie Pearl

37. Who replaced Queensrÿche's guitarist Chris DeGarmo in 1998?
A. Kelly Hanson
B. Kelly Smith
C. Kelly Gray
D. Macy Gray

38. Who replaced Rob Halford as lead singer of Judas Priest?
A. Blaze Bailey
B. Ripper Owens
C. Jeff Scott Soto
D. Mark Walberg

39. Who replaced the original singer of Lillian Axe for their 2007 album?
A. Derrick LeFevre
B. Jaime St. James
C. Jizzy Pearl
D. Mel Torme

40. Who replaced Vinnie Vincent as guitarist for KISS?
A. Bruce Kulick
B. Mark St. John
C. Tommy Thayer
D. Ricky Skaggs

41. Who sang about the "Lord of the Thighs"?
A. Aerosmith
B. Ted Nugent
C. Van Halen
D. Michael Flatley

42. Who sang the song "All Lips 'N Hips"?
A. Electric Boys
B. Bulletboys
C. Tuff
D. Richard Simmons

43. Who stated, "…cockroaches and rats will be the last things on Earth"?
A. Ted Poley
B. Bobbie Blotzer
C. Stephen Pearcy
D. Terminex

44. Who suggested that you "Be Chrool To Your Scuel"?
A. Krokus
B. Alice Cooper
C. Twisted Sister
D. The Beach Boys

45. Who took over singing duties for Quiet Riot when Kevin Dubrow was ousted from the band?
A. Paul Shortino
B. Jizzy Pearl
C. Kevin Chalfant
D. George Clooney

46. Who wanted to "Hold On to 18"?
A. Blue Murder
B. Bombay Black
C. Black 'N Blue
D. Black Panthers

47. Who wanted to "Toke About It"?
A. Motley Crüe
B. LA Guns
C. Tesla
D. The Grateful Dead

48. Who received $1,000,000 to replace Jason Newtead in Metallica?
A. Robert Trujillo
B. Robbie Crane
C. Robert Reed
D. Robbie Rist

49. Who wanted to "Take The Dog Off The Chain"?
A. Savatage
B. Babylon A.D.
C. Vain
D. Not The Catt

50. Who wanted to "Turn up the Radio"?
A. Autograph
B. Loudness
C. XYZ
D. Lawrence Welk

51. Who wanted to get their "Kicks After Six"?
A. Sixx A.M.
B. Kix
C. Scorpions
D. The Synchronized Swimmers

52. Who wanted to throw a knock-down, drag-out, "Rock & Roll Party In The Streets"?
A. Axe
B. Kix
C. L.A. Guns
D. Bert & Ernie

53. Who was brought in to replace Ratt's bass player, Juan Croucier?
A. Jon Levin
B. Robbie Crane
C. Billy Sheehan
D. Bill The Cat

54. Who was going to "Beat the Bullet"?
A. Pretty Maids
B. Vain
C. Helix
D. Curious George

55. Who was NOT a bass player for The Runaways?
A. Jackie Fox
B. Micki Steele
C. Cherry Johnson
D. Vicki Blue

56. Who was *Surfin' with the Alien?*
A. Joe Satriani
B. Steve Vai
C. Steve Morse
D. Steve McQueen

57. Who was the 2nd singer for Anthrax?
A. Joey Belladonna
B. John Bush
C. Scott Ian
D. Joey Tribbiani

58. Who was Ted Nugent's original lead singer, fronting such classics as "Stranglehold" and "Free-For-All"?
A. Ted Nugent
B. Jeff Martin
C. Derek St. Holmes
D. Mount St. Helens

59. Who was the first singer for the Michael Schenker Group?
A. Michael Schenker
B. Jeff Scott Soto
C. Gary John Barden
D. Mr. Green Jeans

60. Who was the lead singer for the Peter Criss/Ace Frehley band CRISS who also sang backup vocals for Jan and Dean as well as The Beach Boys?
A. Paul Stanley
B. Lanny Cordola
C. Philip Bardowell
D. Henrietta Hippo

61. Who was the guest vocalist on the BulletBoys song "Neighborhood" from their 2003 album *Sophie*?
A. Kip Winger
B. Sebastian Bach
C. Kelly Hanson
D. Sophia Loren

62. Who was the original singer of Anthrax?
A. Joey Belladonna
B. John Bush
C. John Connelly
D. George Bush

63. Who was the original singer of Dream Theater?
A. Chris Collins
B. James LaBrie
C. Kevin Moore
D. Michael Moore

64. Who was the original vocalist for Iron Maiden back in the mid '70s?
A. Paul Day
B. Paul Di'Anno
C. Bruce Dickinson
D. Pauly Shore

65. Who was to be the 2nd guitarist in the supergroup Planet Us when Slash decided not to join them?
A. Joe Satriani
B. Steve Howe
C. Trevor Rabin
D. Tiny Tim

66. Who were "Caught in a Mosh"?
A. Anthrax
B. Black Flag
C. Armored Saint
D. Boris Pickett

67. Who were *Leather Boyz With Electric Toyz*?
A. Electric Boys
B. Tuff
C. Pretty Boy Floyd
D. The Village People

68. Who were "Wild in the Streets"?
A. Accept
B. Helix
C. Saxon
D. The Backyardigans

69. Who were on the "Edge of a Broken Heart"?
A. Bitch
B. L7
C. Vixen
D. The Girl Scouts

70. Who were *Screwed, Blued & Tattooed?*
A. Sleeze Beez
B. Motley Crüe
C. Lynch Mob
D. Ron Jeremy

71. Who were the comedy punk-metal band that sang "Three Little Pigs" and had a companion video complete with dope-smoking pigs and a Harley riding big bad wolf?
A. Green Jello
B. Green Jelly
C. Green Jam
D. Mr. Green

72. Who were the "London Leatherboys"?
A. Judas Priest
B. Accept
C. Manowar
D. Wham!

73. Who were the *Strong Arm of the Law?*
A. Saxon
B. Riot
C. Raven
D. Stretch Armstrong

74. Who won the American Music Award in 1990 for "Favorite Heavy Metal/Hard Rock New Artist", beating out both Winger and Warrant?
A. Firehouse
B. Skid Row
C. Trixter
D. Trixters are for Kids

75. Who wrote Rainbow's hit song "Since You Been Gone"?
A. Russ Ballard
B. Richie Blackmore
C. Joe Lynn Turner
D. Frank Hardy

UNA GLEEBIN' GLOPPIN' GLOBBIN'

One of the most successful bands to emerge from the New Wave of British Heavy Metal movement, Def Leppard conquered England then the rest of the world. The Sheffield quintet has overcome numerous obstacles. Two of their guitarists were fired due to alcoholism, with one of them eventually dying from it, followed by the drummer losing his arm in a tragic accident. Yet, the band soldiered on and continued rocking stadiums across the globe. Their most recent tour was in 2022 with Mötley Crüe, Poison, and Joan Jett. They are bona fide rock legends who have sold well over 100 million records.

It wasn't until their third album, 1983's *Pyromania* that they became household names in America thanks to their songs and videos "Photograph," "Foolin,'" and "Rock of Ages." The songs were everywhere. They were on the radio, the television, and even our school bus thanks to the kid who brought his boom box and played the album. Every. Single. Morning. Nonetheless, as young guys in high school we loved the band, their music, and their aesthetic. We even bought our own Union Jack flag. It hung in our room, along with a poster and mirror of the band. Eventually, our concert ticket stubs would be added to the poster.

After endlessly listening to *Pyromania*, we discovered that it wasn't their first album. This led to us going back and buying their previous album, *High 'n' Dry*. Being fans already, our introduction to an even more rockin' album only made us bigger fans.

The rock world waited to see the outcome of the band and its drummer following Rick Allen's horrific car accident. Nobody expected what actually occurred. With the addition of a customized electronic drum kit, Rick Allen continued being the band's sole drummer. Four long years after *Pyromania*, they released their massive follow-up, *Hysteria*. When we first heard the lead single "Women," we weren't sure what to think. It was good but sounded like nothing we had ever heard before. It still rocked but had a unique modern sound. But once the world heard the ballad "Love Bites" and the anthem "Pour Some Sugar on Me," it was clear the band was back and bigger than ever. *Hysteria* went on to sell over twenty-five million copies with six hit singles. The album is still considered one of the greatest rock albums of all time. Although the band never reached the same level of stratospheric success as that album, they have since released many more excellent albums like *Adrenalize* and *Euphoria*, right up through 2022's *Diamond Star Halos*.

As with most of the great "hair metal" bands, we have been fortunate enough to see them in concert many times. The first time was in 1988 when they toured with Tesla and played in the round. But the most memorable show had to be the one in 2003 when I won front-row tickets from a local radio station. Ironically, Don won tickets from the same station a week earlier. Unfortunately for him, his seats were in the back of the stadium. I politely waved to him from the front row, but he was so far away I could only see one finger from his return wave. I think he was just pointing out that I was #1 for being in the first row.

In addition to being an amazing concert, I was able to snag a guitar pick and set list. Securing a $10 bootleg T-shirt in the parking lot on the way out was simply icing on the cake. Or put another way, one more lump of sugar.

CHAPTER 14
EVERYTHING BUT THE KITCHEN SINK
THE PINK

Basically, this final section contains questions about anything and everything. Pretty much nothing is safe at this point. This could contain questions about AC/DC, Zebra, or anything in between. This section has twice as many questions as the other multiple choice questions and is guaranteed to be twice as much fun*.

> * Guarantee is not legally binding in any of the contiguous United States, Alaska, Hawaii, Central America, South America, Antarctica, Europe (the continent, not the band), Asia (the band, not the continent), Africa, Greenland, Iceland, Ice Capades, Ice Castles, Castle Risk, Risky Business, Business Class, First Class, Mercury, Venus, Women are from Mars, Jupiter, Saturn (the planet and the car), Uranus, Ha Ha, I Said Uranus, Pluto (the planet, not the dog) and other planets of the solar federation. We have assumed control. We have assumed control. We have assumed control.

Top: Laughing with another Don
(Jamieson from That Metal Show)
Right: Hanging Loose with Warrant's
Erik Turner

1. "12 O'Clock High" is a song by what band?
A. Def Leppard
B. Odin
C. Europe
D. The Hickory Dickory Docks

2. "If You See Kay" is a cleverly titled song by what band?
A. WASP
B. Helix
C. April Wine
D. Bing Crosby Tap Dancing with Danny Effing Kaye

3. "Miss Mystery" was a hit for what colorful band?
A. Great White
B. Black Sabbath
C. Black 'N Blue
D. Miss Piggy

4. According to the June '06 edition of *Maxim* Magazine which metal singer is ranked #8 on the Top 10 Living Legends of Sex (No, it's not Gene Simmons, he was #3)?
A. Lemmy
B. Bret Michaels
C. David Lee Roth
D. David Allen Coe

5. As of 2022, how many of the 15 Grammy Awards that Joe Satriani has been nominated for has he won?
A. 14
B. 10
C. 0
D. 7

6. At what event did Triumph reunite for the first time in over two decades?
A. Rocklahoma II
B. The Gods 2008
C. 2008 Sweden Rock Festival
D. The Kool Jazz Festival

7. As opposed to guitar picks or drums sticks, what does the Christian metal band Stryper throw out into the crowd at their concerts?
A. Scrolls
B. Condoms
C. Bibles
D. Ouija Boards

8. Attila was a jazz-metal duo featuring Jon Small and what hugely popular artist, both of which were dressed as barbarians on their self-titled, debut album in 1970?
A. Bill Bruford
B. Billy Idol
C. Billy Joel
D. Bilbo Baggins

9. Brothers Dann and David Huff played in what pop metal band who released *Last of the Runaways* in 1989 and had the Top 20 hit "I'll See You in My Dreams"?
A. Tyketto
B. Giant
C. Trixter
D. Runaway

10. BulletBoys guitarist Mick Sweda was formerly the guitarist for what other '80s metal band?
A. King Kobra
B. Europe
C. TNT
D. Slingshot Girls

11. David Letterman's famous drummer and bass player Anton Fig and Will Lee played on what legendary rock guitarist's '78 solo album?
A. Ted Nugent
B. Gene Simmons
C. Ace Frehley
D. Cary Granite

12. Former Ozzy guitarist Jake E. Lee left Ozzy to form what band whose songs included, "Dreams in the Dark" and "Winter's Call"?
A. Bad English
B. Badfinger
C. Badlands
D. Bad Bad Leroy Brown

13. Guitar virtuoso Yngwie Malmsteen was a member of what band featuring Ron Keel on vocals when he came to L.A. in the early '80s.
A. Steeler
B. Alcatrazz
C. San Quentin
D. Peter Paul & Yngwie

14. Heavy metal artists including Black Sabbath, Yes, Rush and Iron Maiden recorded a video compilation to benefit victims of the 1988 earthquake in what country?
A. Chile
B. Armenia
C. Cambodia
D. Middle Earth

15. How many people were in Samantha 7?
A. 7
B. 5
C. 3
D. Pi

16. In 2003, Bon Jovi was nominated for a Grammy for Best Pop Performance by a Duo or Group with Vocal for what song?
A. "Have a Nice Day"
B. "Misunderstood"
C. "I Believe"
D. "Kookaburra"

17. In 2004, Quiet Riot's guitarist Carlos Cavazo teamed up with members of Dio, Lynch Mob and David Lee Roth to form what band?
A. Quiet Riot
B. 3 Legged Dogg
C. 3 Doors Down
D. 3 Piece Chicken Nuggets

18. In 2007, Bon Jovi's new album went to #1. When was the last time they had a #1 album?
A. 1992
B. 2002
C. 1988
D. 1776

19. In the 2005 *The Spongebob Squarepants Movie*, what big hair song's lyrics were modified into Spongebob's song, "I'm a Goofy Goober"?
A. "We're Not Gonna Take It"
B. "I Wanna Rock"
C. "Rock and Roll All Night"
D. "YYZ"

20. Jani Lane, Keri Kelli, Chuck Wright, and Bobby Blotzer teamed up in 2006 to form what project, featuring the songs "Serial Killer", "Bruised", and "Exit"?
A. Angel City Outlaws
B. Contraband
C. Scrap Metal
D. The Killers

21. Metal singer Steve Plunkett wrote the theme song to what popular TV show on the WB network?
A. *Gilmore Girls*
B. *7th Heaven*
C. *Hanna Montana*
D. *Benny Hill*

22. Legendary guitarists Adrian Vandenberg and Vivian Campbell along with Quiet Riot bassist Rudy Sarzo all joined forces in the late '80s playing with what popular metal band?
A. Whitesnake
B. Deep Purple
C. Rainbow
D. The Violent Femmes

23. Name Ace Frehley's song about his 1983 car accident where he repeatedly sings, "…Ace is back and I told you so".
A. "Rocket Ride"
B. "Shock Me"
C. "Rock Soldiers"
D. "Deadman's Curve"

24. Name Guns 'N Roses' first drummer who was ironically dismissed due to substance abuse problems.
A. Duff McKagan
B. Steven Adler
C. Matt Sorum
D. Phil Collins

25. Name Iron Maiden's song about the mythological flyer who got a little too close to the sun.
A. "Run to the Hills"
B. "The Trooper"
C. "Flight of Icarus"
D. "Ouch That's Hot"

26. Name Judas Priest's lead singer *before* Rob Halford.
A. Greg Anderson
B. Ripper Owens
C. Alan Atkins
D. Fred Rogers

27. Name Van Halen's Roth-era producer who followed Diamond Dave when he went solo to produce as well as costar in several of his first videos.

A. Clive Davis
B. Ted Templeman
C. Mutt Lange
D. Simon Cowell

28. Not to be outdone by USA for Africa, what was the name of the group of heavy metal musicians led by Ronnie James Dio who did their own benefit song?

A. Northern Lights
B. Hear 'N Aid
C. USA for Africa
D. Singers Using Care and Kindness (or, SUCK)

29. On which Stryper studio album did American Idol judge Randy Jackson play bass on?

A. *Against The Law*
B. *In God We Trust*
C. *Soldiers Under Command*
D. *Yo, Dawg*

30. Salvation Through Redemption Yielding Peace Encouragement and Righteousness is better known as what?

A. Whiteheart
B. Petra
C. Stryper
D. The Salvation Army

31. The lead singer for the Waitresses, Patty Donahue, appeared on the 1982 album *Zipper Cathches Skin* by what metal artist?

A. Rob Halford
B. Gene Simmons
C. Alice Cooper
D. Ben Stiller

32. The popular rock tune "All The Way To Memphis" was performed by what supergroup consisting of members from Ratt, L.A. Guns and Vixen?
A. Supernova
B. Supergroup
C. Contraband
D. The Beach Boys

33. This hard rock band sang the song "Someone Like You" from their *Psycho Café* album.
A. Kiss
B. Bang Tango
C. Saigon Kick
D. Johnny Horton

34. This metal band got their start opening up for Van Halen on their *1984* tour and had such songs as "Turn Up the Radio" and "My Girlfriend's Boyfriend Isn't Me".
A. Autograph
B. The Cars
C. Warrior Soul
D. Brooks and Dunn

35. Two members of which glam metal band got into a fight backstage at the 1991 *MTV Video Awards*?
A. Hanoi Rocks
B. Motley Crüe
C. Poison
D. Little KISS

36. Vocalist Peppy Castro, keyboardist/vocalist Doug Katsaros and guitarist Bob Kulick (Bruce's brother) made up what early '80s rock band?
A. Balance
B. Firehouse
C. Extreme
D. Firehose

37. What 23 minute Dream Theater song did Mike Portnoy write about the death of his mother?
A. "Another World"
B. "Falling into Infinity"
C. "A Change of Seasons"
D. "As the Butter Churns"

38. What alcoholic drink does Guns N' Roses sing about on their debut LP?
A. Black Tooth Grin
B. Brass Monkey
C. Night Train
D. Shirley Temple

39. What Asian metal band sang the song "Love Junkie"?
A. XYZ
B. EZO
C. Loudness
D. Motorhead

40. What band asked the question, "Oh, You Ate One Too?"
A. Aerosmith
B. Ugly Kid Joe
C. Van Halen
D. Bobby Flay

41. What band did Damn Yankees drummer Michael Cartellone join in 1996 for their *Predator* album?
A. Whitesnake
B. Accept
C. Ratt
D. Anderson, Buttholes, Walkmen & How

42. What band did Yngwie Malmsteen play in with Graham Bonnet of Rainbow and MSG fame?
A. Alcatrazz
B. Steeler
C. Alchemy
D. Altoids

43. What band had the international hit "Midnight in Tokyo" and sang about "Summertime Girls"?
A. Y&T
B. Loudness
C. EZO
D. Pokemon

44. What band observed "Why Is A Carrot More Orange Than an Orange"?
A. Mr. Big
B. Amboy Dukes
C. Damn Yankees
D. Bugs Bunny

45. What band's logo was a punk kid wearing a backwards baseball hat and giving the finger?
A. Motley Crüe
B. Ugly Kid Joe
C. Anthrax
D. Calvin & Hobbes

46. What band's name is prominently displayed on Butt-Head's shirt?
A. Megadeth
B. AC/DC
C. Metallica
D. The Bee Gees

47. What band's debut album is actually called *Assmaster*? No, we aren't making this up!
A. Raging Slab
B. Manowar
C. Trixter
D. Wham!

48. What classic Amboy Dukes tune gets a remake on Ted Nugent's 2007 album?
A. "Journey To The Center Of The Mind"?
B. "Loaded for Bear"
C. "Flight of the Bird"
D. "Rhinestone Cowboy"

49. What classic Grateful Dead song did Tesla pair up with their hit "Comin' Atcha Live" on the first track of their 1990 live album *Five Man Acoustical Jam*?
A. "Truckin'"
B. "Casey Jones"
C. "Uncle John's Band"
D. "Keep On Truckin'"

50. What did Bitch change their name to in 1988 in hopes of more commercial success?
A. Betsy
B. Bitty
C. Vixen
D. Oompa Loompa

51. What did Metallica originally want to call their first album, but their record label wouldn't let them?
A. *Suck My Pick*
B. *Shitload of Metal*
C. *Metal Up Your Ass*
D. *Smell the Glove*

52. What does Bon Scott say at the end of the tune "Night Prowler"?
A. Sit, Ubu, Sit!
B. Shazam!
C. Shazbot, Na-Nu, Na-Nu
D. Somebody Turn On a Night-Light

53. What famous Guns N' Roses song plays at the beginning of Cincinnati Bengals football games?
A. "Sweet Child O' Mine"
B. "Welcome To The Jungle"
C. "Paradise City"
D. "Who Dey Rap"

54. What famous metal band did Randy Rhodes play with before joining Ozzy?
A. Quiet Riot
B. Vanilla Fudge
C. Black Sabbath
D. The Wiggles

55. What former Black Sabbath singer fronted the band Badlands?
A. Ronnie James Dio
B. Joe Lynn Turner
C. Ray Gillen
D. Jimmy Durante

56. What guitar player was brought in to replace Poison's CC DeVille in the early '90s, playing on their *Native Tongue* release?
A. Richie Kotzen
B. Warren DiMartini
C. John Norum
D. Les Paul

57. What guitarist was the original replacement for the late Randy Rhoads for Ozzy's *Blizzard of Oz* tour in 1982?
A. Brad Gillis
B. Bernie Tormé
C. Jake E. Lee
D. Buck Owens

58. What Iron Maiden song came from a Samuel Taylor Coleridge story?
A. "The Rime of the Ancient Mariner"
B. "Flight of Icarus"
C. "Two Minutes to Midnight"
D. "Green Eggs and Ham"

59. What is the name of Mötley Crüe's first album which originally appeared on their own record label but was re-released when they were signed to Elektra.
A. *Livewire*
B. *Too Fast For Love*
C. *Shout At The Devil*
D. *Liposuction*

60. What is the name of the "Little Stevie Vai" song that he plays loudly in front of his class on *Passion and Warfare*, much to the dismay of his teacher who complains, ".. that sounds like noise Mr. Vai…you've all got detention"?
A. "The Audience is Listening"
B. "Passion and Warfare"
C. "Talent Show"
D. "Rubber Duckie"

61. What is the name of the melodic German band featuring Marc Storace, Ralf Heyne, Lars Wilke, and Carsten Witte?
A. Biss
B. Krokus
C. Accept
D. Warsteiner

62. What is the name of the band formed by former Bang Tango front-man Joe Lesté, which signed a major label deal with Warner Brothers Records in 2000?
A. Beautiful Creatures
B. Bombay Black
C. Blanc Faces
D. Dukes of Biohazard

63. What is the name of the two instrumental songs Eddie Van Halen wrote and performed for an adult film in 2006?
A. "Rise" & "Valerie"
B. "Rise" & "Catherine"
C. "Rise" & "Sherry"
D. "Rise" & "Shine"

64. What L.A. metal band featured medieval imagery and was fronted by John Bush before he joined Anthrax?
A. Armored Saint
B. Saxon
C. Manowar
D. Stonehenge

65. What legendary album featured a 1978 painting by Rob T. Williams of a robot raping a woman before it was banned for obvious reasons?
A. *Dressed to Kill*
B. *Toys in the Attic*
C. *Appetite for Destruction*
D. *Short Circuit*

66. What number do you call if you're having trouble with your high school head or you've got problems in your life of love?
A. 24-39-66
B. 867-5309
C. 36-24-36
D. 1-800-Eat Shi*

67. What popular Poison song and video sang about a girl's desperate quest to find Hollywood stardom?
A. "Fallen Angel"
B. "Angel"
C. "Pretty Angel"
D. "Frankenstein"

68. What popular rock band released the strangely titled *Honkin' On Bobo* album?
A. ZZ Top
B. KISS
C. Aerosmith
D. Bozo the Clown

69. What popular Roy Rogers/Dale Evans tune winds up on Van Halen's *Diver Down* album?
A. "That's Life"
B. "You Really Got Me"
C. "Happy Trails"
D. "Trigger Happy"

70. What supergroup consisted of John Waite, Jonathan Cain, Ricky Phillips, Neal Schon, and Deen Castronovo and sang the huge hit "When I See You Smile"?
A. HSAS
B. Damn Yankees
C. Bad English
D. Bad Spanish

71. What TV and motion picture star once auditioned to be the bass player for Helix?
A. Matt Damon
B. George Clooney
C. Michael J. Fox
D. Alf

72. What was the 1990 band featuring Dio alumni Vinny Appice & Tracy G?
A. WWIII
B. White Wolf
C. Warrior Soul
D. Winnie the Pooh and Tigger Too

73. What was the first Ozzy album featuring Jake E. Lee on guitar?
A. *Bark at the Moon*
B. *Diary of a Madman*
C. *Ozzmosis*
D. *Moon the Barking Dog*

74. What was the incredibly popular Mötley Crüe song from *Theater of Pain* which is considered by some as the first power ballad which started the '80s tradition?
A. "Never Say Goodbye"
B. "Don't Go Away Mad (Just Go Away)"
C. "Home Sweet Home"
D. "Grandma Got Run Over By a Reindeer"

75. Who was the lead singer of AC/DC before Bon Scott?
A. Brian Johnson
B. Dave Evans
C. Mark Evans
D. Tom Jones

76. What was the name of Aerosmith's big late '80s comeback album featuring "Dude (Looks Like a Lady)", "Angel" and "Rag Doll"?
A. *Get a Grip*
B. *Permanent Vacation*
C. *Done With Mirrors*
D. *Done With Beers*

77. What was the name of Ace Frehley's big hit from his 1978 solo album, which was written by Russ Ballard and helped his album make it all the way to #13 on the Billboard Hot 100?
A. "Rocket Ride"
B. "New York Groove"
C. "Shock Me"
D. "I Love New York"

78. What was the name of Bad English's 1991 sophmore release?
A. *Bad English II*
B. *Backlash*
C. *Back For More*
D. *Grunge Sucks*

79. What was the name of C.C. DeVille's post-Poison band?
A. Seether
B. 1000 C.C.s
C. Samantha 7
D. Coupe DeVille

80. What was the name of Iron Maiden's drummer before Nicko McBrain?
A. Thunderstick
B. Doug Sampson
C. Clive Burr
D. John Bonham

81. What was the name of Mötley Crüe's female backup singers for the *Girls, Girls, Girls* tour?
A. The Girls, Girls, Girls
B. The Nasty Habits
C. The Naughty Girls
D. The Coral Reefers

82. What was the name of Steve Whiteman's post Kix band?
A. Funny Money
B. Broken Teeth
C. Bombay Black
D. Funny Girl

83. What was the name of Styper's follow-up to their hugely successful album *To Hell With the Devil?*
A. *Against the Law*
B. *Soldiers Under Command*
C. *In God We Trust*
D. *To Yell at the Pebble*

84. What was the name of Tesla's first Top Ten hit, a ballad from their 2nd album *The Great Radio Controversy?*
A. "Signs"
B. "Little Suzi"
C. "Love Song"
D. "Modern Gay Cowboy"

85. What was the name of the 1997 Mötley Crüe album that saw the return of Vince Neil?
A. *New Tattoo*
B. *Generation Swine*
C. *Dr. Feelgood*
D. *Theater of Paint*

86. What was the name of the ABC comedy special where Spinal Tap made their first appearance in 1978?
A. *The TV Show*
B. *The ABC Monday Night Comedy Special*
C. *The 1978 Emmy Awards*
D. *The Nick and Jessica Variety Hour*

87. What was the name of the band that Tony Harnell formed in 1997 with Bruno Ravel?
A. Westworld
B. Danger Danger
C. TNT
D. ABBA

88. What was the name of the late '70s power-trio consisting of Don Dokken, Juan Croucier and Greg Pecka?
A. Dokken
B. Ratt
C. Triumph
D. Dixie Chicks

89. What was the name of the only new song/video from Dokken's live album *Beast From The East?*
A. "Walk Away"
B. "Runaway"
C. "Walkin' Shoes"
D. "Walk Don't Run"

90. What was the name of the song sung by Dio's charity band for African famine relief?
A. "Hearing Aid"
B. "Stars"
C. "Scream"
D. "We are the World"

91. What was the name of the Twisted Sister album where they decided to do away with all of their makeup?
A. *Love Is For Suckers*
B. *Stay Hungry*
C. *Unmasked*
D. *Ugly Mothers*

92. What was the name of the somewhat vertically challenged metal band who ironically sang "Stand Tall (Stick to Your Guns)"?
A. Lilliputians in Leather
B. Killer Dwarfs
C. The Killer Elves
D. The Bilbo Baggins Experience

93. Which classic Judas Priest tune was originally a folk song written by Joan Baez?
A. "Diamonds and Rust"
B. "Victim of Changes"
C. "Sad Wings of Destiny"
D. "I Am Halford, Hear Me Roar"

94. Which Cult song's beginning and guitar driven rhythm sounds nearly identical to AC/DC's "Rock and Roll Singer"?
A. "She Sells Sanctuary"
B. "Wild Flower"
C. "Fire Woman"
D. "The Girl From Ipanema"

95. Which hit Lita Ford song featured the lyric "…had a few beers, gettin' high" which was omitted from the radio version of the song?
A. "Kiss Me Deadly"
B. "Don't Close Your Eyes"
C. "Gotta Let Go"
D. "Yellow Submarine"

96. Which legendary guitarist formerly played in a band called Kantuckee before hitting the big time?
A. Joe Perry
B. Angus Young
C. Eddie Van Halen
D. Hank Williams

97. Which metal legend "went to college" in a popular reality TV series?
A. Tommy Lee
B. Bret Michaels
C. Jani Lane
D. Ben Stein

98. White Lion's drummer Greg D'Angelo was also an early member of what contagious thrash metal band?
A. Overkill
B. Slayer
C. Anthrax
D. Air Supply

99. Who did King Kobra singer Mark Free become after his sex reassignment surgery?
A. Traci Gunn
B. Marcie Free
C. Lita Ford
D. Boy George

100. Who replaced Sebastian Bach as lead singer of Skid Row?
A. Johnny Gioeli
B. Jaime St. James
C. Johnny Solinger
D. Johnny Rotten

101. Who sang "Hammer Swings Down" from their debut self-titled record?
A. Babylon A.D.
B. Shotgun Messiah
C. LA Guns
D. MC Hammer

102. "Love is on the Way" was a popular late '80s heavy metal rock ballad by this band.
A. Tyketto
B. Trixter
C. Saigon Kick
D. Firehose

103. After Thin Lizzy disbanded in 1983, Phil Lynott created a new band by what name?
A. Grand Slam
B. Lizzy Borden
C. Home Run
D. Thick Lizzy

104. Alice Cooper had a hit rock ballad by the same name as a popular glam rock band in the '80s. What was it?
A. "Hanoi Rocks"
B. "Poison"
C. "Cinderella"
D. "Motorheadache"

105. Dream Theater's Mike Portnoy & John Petrucci joined Jordan Rudess and Tony Levin in what experimental band?
A. OSI
B. PPLR
C. Liquid Tension Experiment
D. AC/DC

106. Dream Theater's Petrucci, Myung, and Portnoy all went to what school?
A. Berklee College of Music
B. Cincinnati Conservatory of Music
C. Juilliard
D. Harvard Law School

107. Ex-Hanoi Rocker Sami Yaffa and mohawk wearing Mickey Finn teamed up to form what metal band whose debut album was called *Feel the Shake*?
A. Jetboy
B. Jet
C. Yaffinn
D. UDF

108. Faith No More's lead singer Mike Patton also sang for what other explicit band using the stage name Vlad Drac?
A. Mr. Bungle
B. Peeping Tom
C. Fantomas
D. Mr. Rogers

109. From what planet does Ace Frehley come?
A. Saturn
B. Jendell
C. Melmack
D. Youranus

110. Gil Moore and Mike Levine made up the lesser known 2/3 of what Canadian trio?
A. Rush
B. Triumph
C. King's X
D. Hanson

111. Name Joe Satriani's album in which he finally experimented with adding vocals to several of his typically instrumental tracks.
A. *Flying in a Blue Dream*
B. *Dreaming #11*
C. *The Extremist*
D. *Stick to Playing Guitar*

112. Pink Cream 69's Andy Deris left in 1994 to join what other German metal band?
A. Helloween
B. Accept
C. Bonfire
D. Pink Cream 96

113. Rob Rock, Tommy Aldridge, Rudy Sarzo and Tony MacAlpine were members of what band in 1986?
A. Whitesnake
B. Quiet Riot
C. M.A.R.S.
D. The Rolling Stones

114. Slaughter's Dana Strum and Mark Slaughter were previously members of what other metal band?
A. Vinnie Vincent Invasion
B. Whitesnake
C. Black Sabbath
D. Black Checkers

115. Tesla's song "Song & Emotion" is dedicated to which of their deceased friends?
A. Steve Clark
B. Bon Scott
C. John Bonham
D. Thomas Edison

116. The House Band from the CBS show *Rock Star* backed up what famous singer on his 2006 tour?
A. Ace Frehley
B. Paul Stanley
C. Rober Plant
D. Paul Schaffer

117. The metal band Kix finally achieved some mainstream success in the late '80s with a power ballad, of course. Name it.
A. "Don't Close Your Eyes"
B. "Lie Like a Rug"
C. "Sex"
D. "Macho Man"

118. The Runaways bassist Michael Steele went on to join what popular '80s band?
A. The Blackhearts
B. The Bangles
C. The Lita Ford Band
D. The Yuppie Puppies

119. This metal band successfully remade Alice Cooper's hit "School's Out", replacing "School's been blown to pieces" to "School's closed for recess".
A. Twisted Sister
B. Krokus
C. Skid Row
D. The PTO

120. What band decided to reward a free T-shirt to anyone showing a passport to prove they attended their concert abroad?
A. Manowar
B. Krokus
C. Scorpions
D. Bananarama

121. What band sang about "Rock Candy" and a "Bad Motor Scooter"?
A. Montrose
B. Talas
C. Amboy Dukes
D. Amboy Dukes of Hazzard

122. What band did former KISS guitarist Bruce Kulick form in 1996 with Motley Crüe's former singer John Corabi?
A. Alias
B. Rebel
C. Union
D. Out of a Job

123. What band sang the song "Fly Me Courageous"?
A. Guns 'N Roses
B. Drivin 'N Cryin
C. Huggin' 'N Kissin
D. Poopin' 'N Peeing

124. What band's 1979 demo was called *The Soundhouse Tapes*?
A. Saxon
B. Iron Maiden
C. Metallica
D. Vanilla Pudge

125. What band's 2nd album was finally released 17 years after its debut and featured the song "Ditch the Bitch"?
A. Crashdiet
B. L.A. Guns
C. Johnny Crash
D. Dr. Johnny Fever

126. What city was the center of the '80s metal scene with landmark clubs such as The Whiskey, The Roxy and the Rainbow Bar and Grill ?
A. San Francisco
B. New York
C. L.A.
D. Juno

127. What band's 3rd studio album was called *Size Really Does Matter?*
A. Killer Dwarfs
B. Giant
C. Pretty Boy Floyd
D. Jolly Green Giants

128. What event saw the surviving members of Led Zeppelin reunite for the first time in 1985?
A. Farm Aid
B. Woodstock '94
C. Live Aid
D. Lemon Aid

129. What former Rainbow member teamed up with Yngwie Malmsteen in the late '80s to sing for him on albums such as 1988's *Odyssey?*
A. Joe Lynn Turner
B. Ronnie James Dio
C. Ian Gillan
D. Kelly Clarkson

130. What guitar riff does Pantera include in the live version of "Cowboys from Hell" from their 1997 album *Official Live: 101 Proof?*
A. "Smoke on the Water"
B. "Iron Man"
C. "Cat Scratch Fever"
D. "Tainted Love"

131. What illness has Bret Michaels battled his entire life?
A. Obesity
B. Hypertension
C. Juvenile Diabetes
D. C. C. Deville

132. What is the name of the adult film that Eddie Van Halen wrote and performed two songs for in 2006?
A. *Sacred Skin*
B. *Sacred Sin*
C. *Geisha Girls*
D. *Eat 'Em and Smile*

133. What legendary '70s band did Damn Yankees drummer Michael Cartellone join in the late '90s?
A. Lynard Skynard
B. Foreigner
C. Molly Hatchet
D. Molly Ringwald

134. What metal band wrote the concept album based on the life story of 16th century prophet Nostradamus?
A. Judas Priest
B. Helloween
C. Queensrÿche
D. The Violent Femmes

135. What rock vocalist became the new lead singer for Boston after Brad Delp's untimely passing?
A. Lou Gramm
B. Geoff Tate
C. Michael Sweet
D. Sam Malone

136. What Savatage song led to the formation of the popular Trans-Siberian Orchestra?
A. "24 Hours Ago"
B. "Strange Wings"
C. "Christmas Eve Sarajevo"
D. "Frosty the Snowman"

137. What was Skid Row's hit song about a boy who ends up killing his friend?
A. "Nineteen"
B. "Youth Gone Wild"
C. "18 and Life"
D. "Girls Gone Wild"

138. What was the first AC/DC album ever to debut on the US album charts?
A. *Back in Black*
B. *Black Ice*
C. *For Those About To Rock*
D. *Black & Decker*

139. What was the name of Dream Theater's massive MTV hit from their 1992 album *Images & Words*?
A. "Pull Me Under"
B. "Not Afraid"
C. "Pull Me Over"
D. "Pull My Finger"

140. What was the name of the early '90s band featuring Twisted Sister's Dee Snider, Clive Burr of Iron Maiden and ex-Gillan guitarist Bernie Tormé ?
A. Widowmaker
B. Black Widow
C. Desperado
D. House of Hair

141. What was the name of the Judas Priest tribute band fronted by Ripper Ownes before he actually joined the real band?
A. British Steel
B. Point of Entry
C. Metal Gods
D. Green Menstrual Cycle

142.   What was the name of the guitarist who replaced Randy Rhoads after he left Quiet Riot and also played in Dokken before George Lynch?
A. Carlos Cavazo
B. Greg Leon
C. Jon Levin
D. Pee Wee Herman

143. Where did Johnny Crash members Christopher Steward and August Worchell meet?
A. Prison
B. Boy Scouts
C. Reform school
D. Daisy Scouts

144. Where is the Rock and Roll Hall of Fame located?
A. New York
B. Los Angeles
C. Cleveland
D. Moscow

145. Which 1981 Def Leppard song was remixed with keyboards for the song's 1984 video and turned up on the compact disc version of the album?
A. "Me and My Wine"
B. "Too Late for Love"
C. "Bringin' On the Heartbreak"
D. "Elvira"

146. Which Canadian band was nominated for two Juno Awards, Group of the Year and Album of the Year, in 1984 - 1985?
A. Helix
B. Triumph
C. Honeymoon Suite
D. Musical Youth

147. Which charismatic singer had a short stint as a DJ, replacing Howard Stern when he left terrestrial radio for satellite?
A. Stephen Tyler
B. Gene Simmons
C. David Lee Roth
D. Gary Coleman

148. Which hard rock singer/guitarist was selected to play George Harrison in a production of *Beatlemania*?
A. Aldo Nova
B. Dave Maniketti
C. George Lynch
D. Paul McCartney

149. Which legendary vocalist sang on Yngwie Malmsteen's album *Marching Out*, which featured the popular song "I'll See the Light Tonight"?
A. Jeff Scott Soto
B. Joe Lynn Turner
C. Ian Gillan
D. Debbie Boone

150. Who did Lemmy team up with on the Tammy Wynette hit "Stand By Your Man"?
A. Wendy O. Williams
B. Lita Ford
C. Joan Jett
D. Dolly Parton

151. Who provided the guest singing voice for Spongebob Squarepants in the "Band Geeks" episode where Squidward forms a marching band that sings a classic power ballad-sounding song called "Sweet Victory"?
A. Ted Poley of Danger Danger
B. David Glen Eisely of Giuffria
C. Danny Vaughn of Tyketto
D. Greg Brady of The Silver Platters

Ron & Don Higgins

ROCK AND ROLL AIN'T NOISE POLLUTION

For those about to rock some more trivia, we salute you! AC/DC are the greatest Australian export since Foster's Lager. Calling them legendary seems like an understatement. Iconic seems more appropriate. Even the most casual rock fan knows the familiar riffs and numerous staples of rock radio

From 1975 to 2020, they've released seventeen studio albums, many of which have gone platinum. They've sold over 200 million copies worldwide. Their high energy lead guitarist, Angus Young in a schoolboy uniform is one of the most recognizable rock stars of the last forty plus years. Amazingly, they've not only been around for a long time, but they've continued to be relevant.

Throughout countless world tours they've never turned into a nostalgia act. Consider this. Bon Scott, one of the greatest rock and roll front men of all time, recorded many of their most famous albums, from *High Voltage*, to *Dirty Deeds Done Dirt Cheap* to *Highway to Hell*. And all of them were recorded in the 1970s!

Then in the '80s came two of the biggest albums in rock history, *Back in Black*, followed by the chart-topping *For Those About to Rock*. The 1990s gave us the multi-platinum *The Razors Edge* with the smash hit, "Thunderstruck." Remarkably, in 2008, they once again reached the top of the charts with *Black Ice*. Then, almost 50 years after their first album, they released *Power Up*, containing the hit song "Shot in the Dark."

One of the most incredible things about AC/DC has been their unbelievable resiliency. In 1979 the band released their biggest album to date, *Highway to Hell*. It was the first album of theirs to make it in the top 100 in the US. Soon after they created an album that many consider to be one of the best of all time, their charismatic lead singer tragically died. That would have been the end for most bands; however, AC/DC not only survived they thrived!

Later that year, they released the biggest album of their career. Forty years later tragedy struck again. Founding member Malcolm Young passed away due to dementia, lead singer Brian Johnson had to stop touring because of hearing loss, bassist Cliff Williams retired, and drummer Phil Rudd was arrested for attempted murder! Clearly, AC/DC were finished. Or were they? The lads were able to overcome all these challenges and in 2020 they released the album *Power Up*, which became their third album to debut at number one on the Billboard charts. It is now platinum. Extraordinary!

AC/DC holds a special place in our hearts, not just because we've been fans since first hearing the explosive "TNT," but because the *Flick of the Switch* tour was our first concert and paved the way for our love affair with live music. We still vividly remember rocking out with our high school soccer friends, Steve, Gary, and B.J.. There was a massive crowd, and the air was electric. Thousands of people were air drumming to "Baba O'Reily" when the opening band, Fastway hit the stage. Most of the people stayed seated until the encore when they tore into their biggest hit, "Say What You Will." The place erupted and everyone got to their feet, where they stayed for the rest of the show. Fastway was brilliant and ear-bleedingly loud. Then AC/DC hit the stage and said, "Hold my beer."

ANSWER KEY

Here are the answers for those who may have banged their heads too hard, spent too much time smoking in the boys room or used too much Aqua Net and forgotten them.

CHAP 1

BLOW UP YOUR VIDEO

PAGES 5 - 23

1. "Women"
2. "(Oh) Pretty Woman"
3. "Gotta Let Go"
4. "Rock You Like a Hurricane"
5. "Burning Like a Flame"
6. "One"
7. "Always There For You"
8. "Breaking the Law"
9. "Hot for Teacher"
10. "I Wanna Rock"
11. "The Hunter"
12. "Rainbow in the Dark"
13. Kevin Seal
14. "Shot in the Dark"
15. "Kickstart My Heart"
16. "Contagious"
17. "Who Made Who"
18. "Mama Weer All Crazee Now"
19. "I Wanna Rock"
20. "Not if you was the last immigrant grocer on Earth, honey!"
21. "Body Talk"
22. "Just Like Paradise"
23. "Shandi"
24. "Sweet Child O' Mine"
25. "Heaven's On Fire"
26. "Heaven Sent"
27. "Epic"
28. "Rock and Roll All Night"
29. "Tied Up In Love"
30. "Hot Love"
31. "Smokin' in the Boy's Room"
32. "You're In Love"
33. "Animal"
34. "Bad Medicine"
35. "Crazy Babies"
36. Bobcat Goldthwait
37. "Fool For Your Loving"
38. "Hungry"
39. "Let the Music Do the Talking"
40. "Long Way to Love"
41. "Rock N Roll (Is Gonna Set the Night on Fire)"
42. Vinnie Vincent
43. Waldo
44. Guns 'N Roses
45. "Turbo Lover"
46. "We're Not Gonna Take It"
47. Milton Berle
48. A Twinkie
49. Bobbie Brown
50. Rainy Night
51. "Dr. Feelgood"
52. *Johnny Got His Gun*
53. His Head Explodes
54. J.S. Bach
55. Jessica Hahn
56. Alcatraz

57. Riki Rachtman
58. Ms. Chemistry
59. Pole Position
60. The Five Freedom Fighters
61. Now Maybe They'll See My Side of Things
62. Sam Kinison
63. Private Session
64. Great White's "Once Bitten, Twice Shy"
65. "Freewhell Burnin"
66. Hollywood Taxi
67. Bobby Blotzer
68. The Taste Squad
69. A Glazed Donut
70. Traci Lords
71. MTV2
72. Chucko
73. Jon Bon Jovi & Richie Sambora
74. Femme Fatale
75. Motorhead vs. Pinhead

YOU GIVE LOVE A BAD NAME
CHAP 2
PAGES 24 - 40

1. Joe Satriani
2. Anthrax
3. Saraya
4. Cacumen
5. Myth

6. Heart Attack
7. Roxx Regime
8. Paul
9. Atomic Mass
10. Dennis Wheatley
11. Murray
12. A Russ Meyer movie
13. A flower
14. A band member's relative
15. Kilmister
16. Pesch
17. Van Halen
18. The Dixie Dregs
19. Joker
20. Orc
21. Queensrÿche
22. The Snake
23. Blue Öyster Cult
24. McKinnon
25. City Kidd
26. The Eric Martin Band
27. King's X
28. Adler's Appetite
29. Poison
30. Sammy Hagar
31. Tygers of Pan Tang
32. Lodewijk
33. AC/DC
34. Kix
35. The Lemmys
36. Silver Star

37. Yesterday and Today
38. Black Sabbath
39. Angus Young
40. Bongiovi
41. Nikola
42. Talisman
43. David
44. Bill Z. Bub
45. Zen Lunatic
46. Ian
47. Babyface
48. Mammoth
49. Saxon
50. Ted Nugent
51. Onyx
52. Majesty
53. Fusion
54. Ken
55. 1st Bugs Bunny cartoon
56. Johann
57. Bastard
58. Urchin
59. Hardline
60. Donna D'Errico
61. *Acid Monkey*
62. Cold Gin
63. The Circle
64. Miljenko
65. The Amazing Journey
66. Samson
67. Planet Us

68. Hocus Pocus
69. Her mother's maiden name
70. Anders and Jens Johansson
71. Chip Z'Nuff
72. David Alan Rachtman
73. Motley Crüe
74. Glenn Hughes
75. The Beatles

A.A. MEETING: ARTISTS AND ALBUMS
CHAP 3
PAGES 41 - 50

General

1. *Blackout* – Scorpions
2. *Dirty Rotten Filthy Stinking Rich* – Warrant
3. *Heartbreak Station* – Cinderella
4. *If You Can't Lick 'Em...Lick 'Em* – Ted Nugent
5. *New Jersey* – Bon Jovi
6. *Permanent Vacation* – Aerosmith
7. *Pride* – White Lion
8. *Stay Hungry* – Twisted Sister
9. *The Disregard of Timekeeping* – Bonham
10. *The Final Countdown* – Europe

21st Century Disks

1. *Back To The Rhythm* – Great White

2. *Between the Valley of the Ultra Pussy* – Faster Pussycat
3. *Ordinary Man* – Ozzy Osbourne
4. *Lightning Strikes Again* – Dokken
5. *Love Grenade* – Ted Nugent
6. *Magica* – Dio
7. *Reborn* – Stryper
8. *The Power & The Myth* – House of Lords
9. *The Return of the Great Gildersleeves* – Danger Danger
10. *Waters Rising* – Lillian Axe

Debuts
1. *Breaking the Chains* – Dokken
2. *Don't Touch the Light* – Bonfire
3. *Leather Boys with Electric Toyz* – Pretty Boy Floyd
4. *Lonesome Crow* – Scorpions
5. *Look What the Cat Dragged In* – Poison
6. *Night Songs* – Cinderella
7. *Ready To Strike* – King Kobra
8. *Too Fast for Love* – Motley Crüe
9. *Under The Blade* – Twisted Sister
10. *Wild Cat* – Tygers of Pan Tang

EPs
1. *'74 Jailbreak* – AC/DC
2. *A Change of Seasons* – Dream Theater

3. *A Tale of Sex, Designer Drugs, and the Death of Rock N Roll* – Pretty Boy Floyd
4. *Believe* – Barren Cross
5. *Caution* – Odin
6. *Name Your Poison* – Little Caesar
7. *Power Love* – Lion
8. *Rainmaker* – Iron Maiden
9. *Relativity* – Impellitteri
10. *The Yellow & Black Attack* – Stryper

Solo Efforts
1. *A Fine Pink Mist* – Jake E. Lee
2. *Angel Down* – Sabastian Bach
3. *Capricorn* – Mike Tramp
4. *Collateral Damage* – Ted Poley
5. *Exposed* – Vince Neil
6. *View To a Thrill* – Stephen Pearcy
7. *Songs of Life* – Bret Michaels
8. *Tattooed Millionaire* – Bruce Dickinson
9. *The Usual Suspects* – Joe Lynn Turner
10. *Up From The Ashes* – Don Dokken

Sophomore Releases
1. *7800° Fahrenheit* – Bon Jovi
2. *Break Like The Wind* – Spinal Tap

3. *Cocked and Loaded* – L.A. Guns

4. *The Great Radio Controversy* – Tesla

5. *Menace to Sobriety* – Ugly Kid Joe

6. *Over The Edge* – Hurricane

7. *Strength in Numbers* – Tyketto

8. *Tangled in Reins* – Steelheart

9. *Open Up and Say...Ahh!* – Poison

10. *Wake Me When It's Over* – Faster Pussycat

Live Albums

1. *Alive II* – KISS

2. *Beast from the East* – Dokken

3. *Fire and Gasoline* – Krokus

4. *Hotter Than Hell Live!* – Barren Cross

5. *Intensities in 10 Cities* – Ted Nugent

6. *Live After Death* – Iron Maiden

7. *Live At The Roxy - Wake Up Bitch* – Pretty Boy Floyd

8. *Made in Japan* – Deep Purple

9. *Unleashed in the East* – Judas Priest

10. *Vitamins and Crash Helmets Tour-Live Greatest Hits* – Dangerous Toys

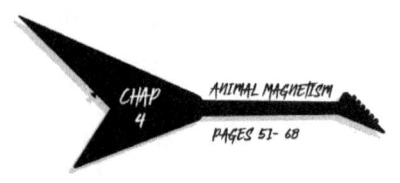

CHAP 4

ANIMAL MAGNETISM

PAGES 51- 68

1. Coney Hatch

2. Aldo Nova

3. Metallica

4. Lion

5. Black Sabbath

6. Udo Dirkschneider

7. Another Animal

8. Dokken

9. Mickey Ratt

10. Vivian Campbell

11. *Wicked Sensation*

12. Eddie Van Halen

13. Great White

14. Train Station

15. Cinderella

16. Hamster

17. Scorpions

18. Bulletboys

19. Pete Willis

20. Tawny Kitaen

21. "Switch 625"

22. Krokus

23. Vyper

24. Dokken

25. The Sharks

26. The Moon

27. Zebra

28. Scorpions
29. Brazil
30. Voivod
31. Cats in Boots
32. Tyger Tyger
33. Leatherwolf
34. Jetland
35. Michael Schenker
36. Rough Cutt
37. Sin Dizzy
38. Helix
39. Whitefoxx
40. Dreamer
41. Riverdogs
42. Babylon A.D.
43. We Are Sexual Perverts
44. Ted Poley
45. Reggie Wu
46. Rick Allen
47. Bourgeois Pigs
48. Raya Beam
49. Tim McGraw
50. Tawny Kitaen
51. Richie Sambora
52. Glenn Hughes
53. Blue Murder
54. Helloween
55. Don Dokken
56. King Kobra
57. Alice Cooper
58. *...Twice Shy*

59. *Subject*
60. Beau Hill
61. Cathouse Club
62. Marshal Berle
63. Tyger Tyger
64. Fashion Rock
65. Saraya
66. Y&T
67. Accept
68. Robbin Crosby
69. Reb Beach
70. "Photograph"
71. *Saints and Sinners*
72. Jizzy Pearl
73. Rhino Bucket
74. Jon Bon Jovi
75. Lemmy

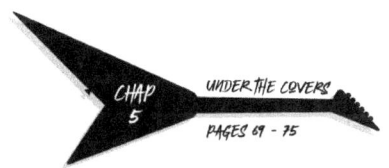

CHAP 5

UNDER THE COVERS

PAGES 69 - 75

Rock Hard

1. "That's Life" - David Lee Roth
   – Frank Sinatra
2. "Helter Skelter" - Motley Crüe
   – The Beatles
3. "I Can't Explain" - The Who
   – Scorpions
4. "Hard Luck Woman" – KISS
   – Garth Brooks

5. "The Real Me" - The Who
– W.A.S.P.

6. "Cat's in the Cradle" - Harry Chapin – Ugly Kid Joe

7. "Radar Love" - Golden Earring – White Lion

8. "Crash Course in Brain Surgery" - Metallica – Budgie

9. "Wild Thing" - Sam Kinison – The Troggs

10. "Don't Be Cruel" - Elvis Presley – Cheap Trick

11. "Ballroom Blitz" – Sweet – Krokus

12. "Do Ya" - E.L.O. – Ace Frehley

13. "Signs" – Tesla – Five Man Electrical Band

14. "Anarchy in the U.K." - Sex Pistols – Mötley Crüe

15. "Smokin' In The Boys Room" - Mötley Crüe – Brownsville Station

Harder Rock

1. "Rock Candy" – Montrose – Bulletboys

2. "Cover of the Rolling Stone" - Dr. Hook – Poison

3. "Once Bitten, Twice Shy" – Great White – Ian Hunter

4. "Bloodstone" – Judas Priest – Stratovarius

5. "All The Way From Memphis" – Mott the Hoople – Contraband

6. "The Green Manalishi" - Judas Priest – Fleetwood Mac

7. "Shining Star" – Earth, Wind & Fire – Stryper

8. "Piece of my Heart" – Janis Joplin – Rough Cutt

9. "Your Mama Don't Dance" – Poison – Loggins and Messina

10. "Stayed Awake All Night" – Krokus – Bachman Turner Overdrive

11. "Leader of the Pack" – Twisted Sister – Shangri-Las

12. "Parasite" – KISS – Anthrax

13. "Because the Night" – Patti Smith – Keel

14. "You're So Vain" – Carly Simon – Faster Pussycat

15. "Let The Music Do The Talking" – Aerosmith – The Joe Perry Project

Little Blue Pill

1. "Tobacco Road" – John D. Loudermilk – David Lee Roth

2. "A Whiter Shade of Pale" – Procol Harum – HSAS

3. "Hot Cherie" – Danny Spanos – Hardline

4. "Antisocial" – Antrhax – Trust

5. "Love is All Around" (Mary Tyler Moore show theme) – Sonny Curtis – Joan Jett & the Blackhearts
6. "Little Suzi" – Tesla – PhD
7. "New York Groove" – Ace Frehley – Hello
8. "God Gave Rock and Roll to You" – Argent – KISS
9. "Since You've Been Gone" – Russ Ballard – Impellitteri
10. "Walking the Dog" – Aerosmith/Ratt – Rufus Thomas

Cover Albums
1. *$5.98 EP: Garage Days Re-revisited* – Metallica
2. *Feedback* – Rush
3. *Metal Jukebox* – Helloween
4. *Poison'd* – Poison
5. *Real to Reel* – Tesla
6. *Take Cover* – Queensrÿche
7. *The Hitlist* – Joan Jett
8. *The Spaghetti Incident?* – Guns N' Roses
9. *Under Cover* – Ozzy
10. *Yeah!* – Def Leppard

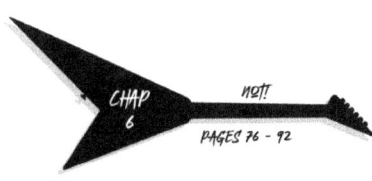

CHAP 6 not!
PAGES 76 - 92

1. *Metaphysical Graffiti*

2. Last Autumn's Dream
3. Megadeth
4. The Angels
5. Motley Crüe
6. Spade Thomas
7. Deep Purple
8. Tyketto
9. UFO
10. Warrant
11. Quiet Riot
12. Iron Maiden
13. Crane
14. The Raspberries
15. Tora Tora
16. Whitesnake
17. Blanc Faces
18. Velvet Revolver
19. Aerosmith
20. Babylon A.D.
21. Black Sabbath
22. Bombay Black
23. Firehouse
24. Warrant
25. Winter
26. Jasmine
27. *Sabotage*
28. Waysted
29. Dokken
30. Black Sabbath
31. Tesla
32. The Cult

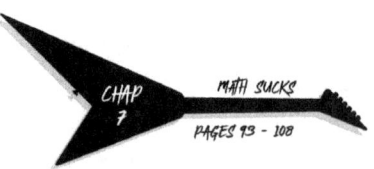

CHAP 7   MATH SUCKS   PAGES 93 - 108

14. Rainbow
15. TMG
16. Last Autumn's Dream
17. Black Sabbath
18. Katmandu
19. The Firm
20. Demons & Wizards
21. The Dudes of Wrath
22. Hookers and Blow
23. Adler's Appetite
24. Velvet Revolver
25. L.A. Guns
26. HSAS
27. Alias
28. Saints of the Underground
29. The Untouchables
30. Iconic
31. Big Noize
32. Blue Murder
33. Revolution Saints
34. Seventh Key
35. Unruly Child
36. Platypus
37. Union
38. 100 Proof
39. White Lion
40. Samson
41. Planet Us
42. Rock Star Supernova
43. Brides of Destruction
44. Fastway

45. Scrap Metal
46. Mother's Army
47. Steel Dragon
48. UFO
49. Black Swan
50. Impelliteri
51. Sunstorm
52. The End Machine
53. Westworld
54. Damnocracy
55. Keel
56. Damn Yankees
57. Melodica
58. The Runaways
59. "Wild Thing"
60. Starbreaker
61. China Blue
62. M.A.R.S.
63. US 66
64. The Winery Dogs
65. King's X
66. Lion
67. Damage Control
68. Waysted
69. Chickenfoot
70. Cactus
71. The Big Ball Stars
72. Jelly Jam
73. The Mob
74. Black Country Communion
75. Four Horsemen

CHAP 8

CAT MATCH FEVER
PAGES 109 - 115

Drummers

1. Carmine Appice – Blue Murder
2. Eric Singer – KISS/Badlands
3. Frankie Banali – Quiet Riot
4. Herman Rarebell – Scorpions
5. Jimmy Chalfant – Kix
6. Michael Cartellone – Damn Yankees
7. Mike Portnoy – Dream Theater
8. Pat Torpey – Mr. Big
9. Troy Luccketta – Tesla
10. Vinny Appice – Black Sabbath

Singers

1. Bob Catley – Magnum
2. Brian Vollmer – Helix
3. Corey Glover – Living Colour
4. Danny Vaughn – Tyketto
5. Dave Meniketti – Y&T
6. David Glen Eisely – Giuffria
7. David St. Hubbins – Spinal Tap
8. Doro Pesch – Warlock
9. Jack Russell – Great White
10. Jaime St. James – Black 'N' Blue
11. James Christian – House of Lords
12. Jason McMaster – Dangerous Toys
13. Jeff Keith – Tesla
14. Kelly Hansen – Hurricane
15. Marc Storace – Krokus
16. Marq Torien – Bullet Boys
17. Michael Matijevic – Steelheart
18. Michael Sweet – Stryper
19. Paul Shortino – Rough Cutt
20. Pete Loran – Trixter
21. Phil Lewis – L.A. Guns
22. Spike – Quireboys
23. Steve Plunkett – Autograph
24. Steve Summers – Pretty Boy Floyd
25. Steve Whiteman – Kix
26. Taime Downe – Faster Pussycat
27. Ted Poley – Danger Danger
28. Tom Keifer – Cinderella
29. Tony Harnell – TNT
30. Whitfield Crane – Ugly Kid Joe

Guitarists

1. Andy Timmons – Danger Danger
2. Billy Sheehan – Talas
3. Brent Muscrat – Faster Pussycat
4. Carlos Cavazo – Quiet Riot
5. Chris DeGarmo – Queensrÿche
6. Chris Holmes – W.A.S.P.
7. Jay Jay French – Twisted Sister
8. John Norum – Europe
9. John Sykes – Blue Murder

10. Mark Kendall – Great White
11. Paul Gilbert – Mr. Big
12. Pete Lesperance – Harem Scarem
13. Ronni LeTekro – TNT
14. Steve Blaze – Lillian Axe
15. Ted Nugent – Damn Yankees
16. Tommy Skeoch – Tesla
17. Ty Tabor – King's X
18. Vernon Reid – Living Colour
19. Vito Bratta – White Lion
20. Warren DeMartini – Ratt

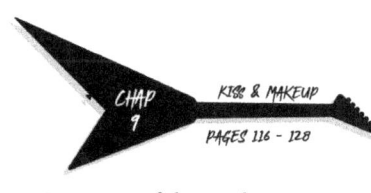

CHAP 9 — KISS & MAKEUP — PAGES 116 - 128

1. *Creatures of the Night*
2. Gene Simmons
3. The Cat Club
4. Warrior
5. Peter Criss
6. Frehley's Comet
7. White Tiger
8. Eric Carr
9. *Smashes, Thrashes and Hits*
10. Blackjack
11. Angel
12. Wicked Lester
13. The Criss/Penridge Alliance
14. Israel

15. *Animalize*
16. Flasher
17. *Dynasty*
18. *Lick it Up*
19. Eric Singer
20. *Revenge*
21. Mötley Crüe
22. Vinnie Vincent Invasion
23. House of Lords
24. Helix
25. "God of Thunder"
26. The KISS Army
27. A rose
28. 3
29. Casablanca
30. "Shock Me"
31. *Family Jewels*
32. *Carnival of Souls*
33. *Dynasty*
34. *(Music From) The Elder*
35. *Psycho Circus*
36. *Village Voice*
37. The Duckies
38. Ankh Warrior
39. *Double Platinum*
40. Vinnie Vincent
41. *Unmasked*
42. *Creatures of the Night*
43. Bruce Kulick
44. Peter Criss
45. Peter Criss

46. Ace

47. "Hide Your Heart"

48. Anton Fig

49. Vinnie Vincent

50. Tommy Thayer

CHAP 10 — SRM: SONGS & MUSICIANS — PAGES 129 - 136

Christmas

1. "Christmas Time Again"
   – Extreme
2. "Everyday Should Be Like Christmas" – Bullet Boys
3. "Father Christmas" – Warrant
4. "Happy Christmas (War Is Over)" – Winger
5. "Heavy Metal Christmas (The Twelve Days Of Christmas)" – Twisted Sister
6. "I Saw Mommy Kissing Santa Claus" – Gilby Clarke
7. "Naughty Naughty Christmas" – Danger Danger
8. "Rockin' Around the Christmas Tree" – Firehouse
9. "Run Rudolph Run" – L.A. Guns
10. "Santa Claus is Coming To Town" – Dokken

11. "Santa's Back In Town" – Roxx Gang
12. "Silent Night" – Faster Pussycat
13. "White Christmas" – Queensrÿche
14. "Winter Wonderland" – Stryper
15. "Won't Be Home For Xmas" – Every Mother's Nightmare

Instrumentals

1. "Battle Axe" – Quiet Riot
2. "D.T." – AC/DC
3. "Eruption" – Van Halen
4. "Sapphire" – TNT
5. "Serenade To The Court" – Odin
6. "The Inevitable Summer" – Dream Theater
7. "Freedom to Fly" – Tony MacAlpine
8. "Molto Arpeggiosa" – Yngwie J. Malmsteen's Rising Force
9. "Stained Mirror" – Riot
10. "The Call of Ktulu" – Metallica

Power Ballads

1. "Don't Know What You Got (Till It's Gone)" – Cinderella
2. "Headed for a Heartbreak" – Winger

3. "Heaven" – Warrant
4. "Is This Love" – Whitesnake
5. "When The Children Cry" – White Lion
6. "Bad For Each Other" – Shark Island
7. "Don't Close Your Eyes" – Kix
8. "Home Sweet Home" – Motley Crüe
9. "Honestly" – Stryper
10. "House of Pain" – Faster Pussycat
11. "I Wanna Be With You" – Pretty Boy Floyd
12. "Out of Love" – Blue Murder
13. "This Time" – Sleeze Beez
14. "To Be With You" – Mr. Big
15. "The Ballad of Jayne" – L.A. Guns

Heavy Metal Chicks
1. "Can I Sit Next To You Girl" – AC/DC
2. "Carrie" – Europe
3. "Charlotte the Harlot" – Iron Maiden
4. "Christine Sixteen" – KISS
5. "Heavy Metal Love" – Helix
6. "Little Suzi" – Tesla
7. "Madelaine" – Winger

8. " Magdalaine" – L.A. Guns
9. "Only Women Bleed" – Alice Cooper
10. "Shotgun Sally" – Cats in Boots

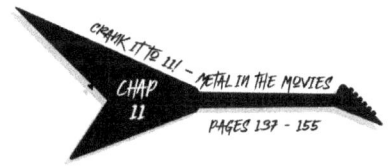

CRANK IT TO 11! – METAL IN THE MOVIES
CHAP 11
PAGES 137 - 155

1. Joan Jett
2. Pantera
3. Iron Maiden
4. Lion
5. *Friday the 13th (Part VI)*
6. *Shocker*
7. *Black Roses*
8. *The Hulk*
9. *Wayne's World*
10. *Young Guns II*
11. *Interview with the Vampire*
12. Steve Vai
13. *Pee Wee's Big Adventure*
14. *Terminator 2*
15. *Anuk-The Path of the Warrior*
16. *Airheads*
17. *This Is Spinal Tap*
18. Dudes of Wrath
19. *Runaway*
20. *Over the Top*
21. *Shocker*
22. *Bill and Ted's Excellent Adventure*

23. Metallica
24. Lenny from *Laverne & Shirley*
25. *The Karate Kid, Part III*
26. *Dudes*
27. *Say Anything*
28. *Endless Love*
29. *A Star is Born*
30. *The SpongeBob SquarePants Movie*
31. *End of Days*
32. *Spider-Man*
33. *Point Break*
34. Steelheart
35. The Folksmen
36. *Goulies II*
37. *Heavy Metal*
38. The Runaways
39. Martin Sheen
40. *Rock Star*
41. Lion
42. Vinnie Vincent Invasion
43. "Time Machine"
44. *Bill & Ted's Bogus Journey*
45. Eddie Van Halen
46. *Roadie*
47. Penelope Spheeris
48. *Airheads*
49. *House of Eternity*
50. Odin
51. Blood Pollution
52. *Better Off Dead*
53. Dokken
54. Fastway
55. Helix
56. Ron Keel
57. *Tenacious D in The Pick of Destiny*
58. *Buffy the Vampire Slayer*
59. Heavy Metal
60. "We all Die Young"
61. *The Money Pit*
62. *Metal God*
63. *The Song Remains The Same*
64. *Heavy Metal Parking Lot*
65. *Eat the Rich*
66. *Detroit Rock City*
67. *A Letter From Death Row*
68. *KISS Meets the Phantom of the Park*
69. *The Decline of Western Civilization Part II: The Metal Years*
70. Steel Dragon
71. Izzy
72. Pretty Boy Floyd
73. Gene Simmons
74. *Maximum Overdrive*
75. *Led Zeppelin IV*

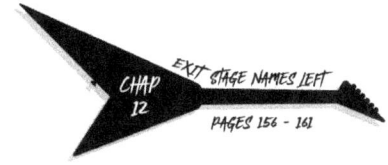

CHAP 12   EXIT STAGE NAMES LEFT   PAGES 156 - 161

Nicknames

3. Diamond Dave – David Lee Roth
8. Bonzo – John Bonham
2. Wacko – Rob Hunter
5. Dimebag – Darrell Abbott
7. Fast – Eddie Clarke
6. Fingers – Eddie Ojeda
13. King – Robbin Crosby
1. Nicko – Michael Henry McBrain
9. Philthy Animal – Phil Taylor
11. Sex – Steve Summers
10. Steamin' – Steve Clark
12. The Animal – Mark Mendoza
4. The King of All Badasses
 – Dave Evans
15. Ripper – Tim Owens
14. Woop – Jeff Warner

Stage Names

1. Alice Cooper – Vincent Furnier
2. Axl Rose – William Bailey
3. Bobby Dall – Robert Harry Kuykendall
4. Buckethead – Brian Carroll
5. Bumblefoot – Ron Thal
6. C.C. Deville – Bruce Anthony Johannesson
7. Cozy Powell – Colin Flooks
8. Eric Carr – Paul Caravello
9. Gene Simmons – Chaim Witz
10. Izzy Stradlin – Jeffrey Dean Isbell
11. Jake E. Lee – Jakey Lou Williams
12. Jizzy Pearl – Jim Wilkinson
13. Joe Lynn Turner – Joseph Linquito
14. Joey Belladonna – Joseph Bellardini
15. Mark St. John – Mark Norton
16. Mick Mars – Robert Deal
17. Nikki Sixx – Frank Feranna, Jr.
18. Paul Stanley – Stanley Eisen
19. Rachel Bolan – James Southworth
20. Razzle – Nicholas Dingley
21. Rikki Rockett – Richard Allan Ream
22. Ronnie James Dio – Ronald Padavona
23. Saraya – Sandi Salvador
24. Slash – Saul Hudson
25. Bret Micheals – Bret Sychak
26. Timothy Gaines – Timothy Hagelganz
27. Tommy Lee – Thomas Bass
28. Tracii Guns – Tracy Ulrich
29. Vince Neil – Vincent Wharton

30. Vinnie Vincent – Vincent Cusano

CHAP 13
WHO THE F*&# ARE YOU?
PAGES 162 - 177

1. Tony Mills
2. Robert Fleischman
3. Bruce Dickinson
4. Ronnie James Dio
5. Warlock
6. Pretty Boy Floyd
7. Steelheart
8. Paul Black
9. Junkyard
10. Mr. Big
11. RIOT
12. Ugly Kid Joe
13. Glenn Hughes
14. Herman Rarebell
15. Diamond Darrell
16. Sister Mary
17. Shannon Tweed
18. Danny Vaughn
19. Justin Hawkins
20. Tommy Lee
21. Rob Halford
22. Dee Snider
23. Jerry Cantrell
24. Jorn Lande
25. Jon Bon Jovi
26. Jason Bonham
27. Kirk Hammett
28. Gene Simmons
29. Sam Kinison
30. Carmine Appice
31. Vinnie Vincent
32. Janick Gers
33. Blaze Bayley
34. Jordan Rudess
35. Jimmy Crespo
36. Reb Beach
37. Kelly Gray
38. Ripper Owens
39. Derrick LeFevre
40. Mark St. John
41. Aerosmith
42. Electric Boys
43. Stephen Pearcy
44. Twisted Sister
45. Paul Shortino
46. Black 'N Blue
47. Tesla
48. Robert Trujillo
49. Babylon A.D.
50. Autograph
51. Scorpions
52. Axe
53. Robbie Crane
54. Vain
55. Cherry Johnson

56. Joe Satriani
57. Joey Belladonna
58. Derek St. Holmes
59. Gary John Barden
60. Philip Bardowell
61. Sebastian Bach
62. John Connelly
63. Chris Collins
64. Paul Day
65. Joe Satriani
66. Anthrax
67. Pretty Boy Floyd
68. Helix
69. Vixen
70. Sleeze Beez
71. Green Jelly
72. Accept
73. Saxon
74. Skid Row
75. Russ Ballard

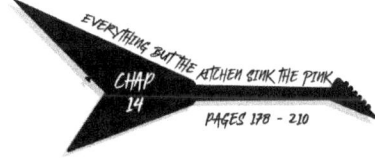

1. Odin
2. April Wine
3. Black 'N Blue
4. Lemmy
5. 0
6. 2008 Sweden Rock Festival
7. Bibles
8. Billy Joel
9. Giant
10. King Kobra
11. Ace Frehley
12. Badlands
13. Steeler
14. Armenia
15. 3
16. "Misunderstood"
17. 3 Legged Dogg
18. 1988
19. "I Wanna Rock"
20. Angel City Outlaws
21. "7th Heaven"
22. Whitesnake
23. "Rock Soldiers"
24. Steven Adler
25. "Flight of Icarus"
26. Alan Atkins
27. Ted Templeman
28. Hear 'N Aid
29. *Against The Law*
30. Stryper
31. Alice Cooper
32. Contraband
33. Bang Tango
34. Autograph
35. Poison
36. Balance
37. "A Change of Seasons"

38. Night Train
39. EZO
40. Van Halen
41. Accept
42. Alcatrazz
43. Y&T
44. Amboy Dukes
45. Ugly Kid Joe
46. AC/DC
47. Raging Slab
48. "Journey To The Center Of The Mind"?
49. "Truckin'"
50. Betsy
51. *Metal Up Your Ass*
52. Shazbot, Na-Nu, Na-Nu
53. "Welcome To The Jungle"
54. Quiet Riot
55. Ray Gillen
56. Richie Kotzen
57. Bernie Tormé
58. "The Rime of the Ancient Mariner"
59. *Too Fast For Love*
60. "The Audience is Listening"
61. Biss
62. Beautiful Creatures
63. "Rise" & "Catherine"
64. Armored Saint
65. *Appetite for Destruction*
66. 36-24-36

67. "Fallen Angel"
68. Aerosmith
69. "Happy Trails"
70. Bad English
71. Michael J. Fox
72. WWIII
73. *Bark at the Moon*
74. "Home Sweet Home"
75. Dave Evans
76. *Permanent Vacation*
77. "New York Groove"
78. *Backlash*
79. Samantha 7
80. Clive Burr
81. The Nasty Habits
82. Funny Money
83. *In God We Trust*
84. "Love Song"
85. *Generation Swine*
86. *The TV Show*
87. Westworld
88. Dokken
89. "Walk Away"
90. "Stars"
91. *Love Is For Suckers*
92. Killer Dwarfs
93. "Diamonds and Rust"
94. "Wild Flower"
95. "Kiss Me Deadly"
96. Angus Young
97. Tommy Lee

98. Anthrax

99. Marcie Free

100. Johnny Solinger

101. Babylon A.D.

102. Saigon Kick

103. Grand Slam

104. "Poison"

105. Liquid Tension Experiment

106. Berklee College of Music

107. Jetboy

108. Mr. Bungle

109. Jendell

110. Triumph

111. *Flying in a Blue Dream*

112. Helloween

113. M.A.R.S.

114. Vinnie Vincent Invasion

115. Steve Clark

116. Paul Stanley

117. "Don't Close Your Eyes"

118. The Bangles

119. Krokus

120. Manowar

121. Montrose

122. Union

123. Drivin 'N Cryin

124. Iron Maiden

125. Johnny Crash

126. L.A.

127. Pretty Boy Floyd

128. Live Aid

129. Joe Lynn Turner

130. "Cat Scratch Fever"

131. Juvenile Diabetes

132. *Sacred Sin*

133. Lynard Skynard

134. Judas Priest

135. Michael Sweet

136. "Christmas Eve Sarajevo"

137. "18 and Life"

138. *Black Ice*

139. "Pull Me Under"

140. Desperado

141. British Steel

142. Greg Leon

143. Reform school

144. Cleveland

145. "Bringin' On the Heartbreak"

146. Helix

147. David Lee Roth

148. Aldo Nova

149. Jeff Scott Soto

150. Wendy O. Williams

151. David Glen Eisely of Giuffria

ACKNOWLEDGEMENTS

We would like to thank:

First and foremost we would like to thank our publisher, Melissa Carrigee. Your belief, hard work, and commitment to this project has been a blessing. You have taken our dream and turned it into a reality. We truly appreciate all you have done for us. We would also like to thank Martha Quinn (yes, that Martha Quinn). It was through our following of her Facebook page that we discovered Melissa and Small Town Girl publishing. Martha asked an interesting question about podcasts and Melissa responded and mentioned that she was starting a new '80s-focused imprint. Contact was made and the rest, as they say, is history. We would also like to thank all of the artists who we've listened to and enjoyed over the years, many of which we have been fortunate enough to see live, from our first AC/DC concert in 1983 to the Raven concert we saw last week and the hundreds of ones in between. This includes world famous acts Def Leppard and Scorpions to lesser-known acts like Lillian Axe and Heaven's Edge as well a great regional acts like Prizoner, Ice Water Mansion and The Take. We also wish to thank our family and friends who have joined us on our many concert escapades. Whether it was Peter and Reyna road-tripping to Detroit for the Scorpions show, Mike driving us to Atlanta to see Stratovarius, Tom joining us at many KISS shows, or Russell who's always willing to check out a band, even one's he's never heard of like Anvil, Diamond Head, Raven and Riot Act! And we have to send a special thank you to our amazing parents, who have always been supportive of all our various endeavors as well as introducing us to music at an early age. Mom has always been a huge Elvis fan and Dad loves Big Band music and always had the radio on growing up. Granted, back in the '70s it was often AM radio, but we discovered the FM frequency soon enough and spent hours holding a tape recorder next to the radio to capture the magical sounds emitting from its speakers!

Ron would also like to thank:

I would like to thank my wife Lynda of 27 years for tolerating my live music obsession and holding down the fort while I'm out rocking and rolling. I know it's not always easy, especially after we went from a family of five to a family of eight after the adoption. But we're all lucky to have you and you've always supported my dreams to be a published author. I still think you should pursue writing as well because you're very talented. Your family and friends agree. Speaking of family, I've enjoyed attending concerts with my in-laws, nieces, nephews, cousins, and others. And I love that I've passed along my love of live music to my kids. I took Carter to see INXS for his first show and more recently saw The Struts with him, Rylie, Evan and (much to his dismay) Chase. Evan's first show was KISS (in full make-up) and we enjoyed seeing Y&T before the pandemic started. He is himself a musician and has mastered the art of snagging set lists, picks and drum sticks as have my other kids. Jack and Aiden – you're next! As a Christian, I would also be remiss if I didn't give thanks to the Good Lord above. I have been blessed beyond measure. And finally, I'd like to thank Don for being my musical partner, whether it's going to shows together or writing this book. We've attended nearly every show together and we both share the same love of music. It's almost like we're twins or something!

Don would also like to thank:

I'd like to thank my parents and my kids for sharing my love of music. All three are decent musicians and have also accompanied me to numerous concerts. Hannah who went with me to her first Buffett concert on her first day of kindergarten as well as some more recent rock concerts. Zane who first saw Styx and REO Speedwagon with me and who constantly battles with me on what to play on the radio in the car. His musical taste isn't exactly the same as mine but as long as we're listening to something together, it's all good. And my oldest son Ethan, who's been to the most rock concerts with me, from Kiss, Prizoner and the Beach Boys, to the Yes *Close to the Edge* 50th anniversary tour we just came from tonight. It's always an adventure. Also other family members who've been to shows with me: Kim, Kelly, Tony, Lynda, Carter, Evan, Alexy and Avery. And finally, I'd like to thank Ron for being my best friend and sharing my love of music. He really took the lead on this project and has partnered with me on some other writing projects and various Fred and Barney schemes (stay tuned world)!